Textual Criticism of the Old Testament

The Septuagint after Qumran

by
Ralph W. Klein

Ⅎ

Fortress Press

Philadelphia

To Marilyn
And the Students of
Christ Seminary—Seminex

Library of Congress Catalog Card Number 74-80420

ISBN 0-8006-1087-3

Second printing 1978

7066A78   Printed in the United States of America   1-1087

Editor's Foreword

The first three volumes in this series introduced methods of biblical scholarship which might generally be called literary approaches. Literary criticism, form criticism, and tradition history attempt to reconstruct the history and the pre-history of the growth of the Old Testament literature and to interpret its meaning in various contexts. None of these methods is fully adequate when used alone; each focuses upon the biblical material from a particular point of view and pursues a certain course of inquiry. The interpreter is aware that these procedures must be used in conjunction with one another and with other methods as well. With the present volume the scope of the series is expanded to include one of those other methods.

Textual criticism, the oldest of the critical disciplines of biblical scholarship, aims at recovering the original copies of the biblical books. But textual criticism is essential precisely because none of those original copies any longer exists, and all subsequent texts are more or less "corrupt"; that is, they all diverge from the original to some extent. Since such original copies are no longer available the best text must be reconstructed by comparing the extant texts with one another.

As the textual critic pursues his task, the question is not whether a particular text or manuscript is reliable or not, but wherein its reliability lies. Every text is conditioned by its historical circumstances and by the fact that it stands at a particular point in the process of transmission. Even the King James version is a reliable translation for understanding a very late stage in this history, reflecting the language, linguistic skills, and the state of textual criticism in the seventeenth century. Because all texts and versions of the Bible are historically conditioned documents, textual criticism must not only try to recover the best text but also attempt to reconstruct the history of the transmission of texts and versions. In this sense, textual criticism addresses another aspect of the question explored by literary, form, and tradition criticism: what course did the history of the Bible take? It is not possible to distinguish sharply between the stages of that history which are treated respectively by the various methods. For example, this book examines some points where questions of textual transmission overlap with issues of redaction (history of composition) in ways which had only been suspected until recently but now can be shown with clarity.

This volume introduces the methods of textual criticism, shows by example how it operates, and summarizes some of the more important results of recent research in the discipline. Toward the ends of reconstructing the best text and writing the history of the transmission of the biblical text theories must be proposed and tested. So this volume presents and illustrates some basic theories, particularly concerning the history of the Greek versions and their relationship to the Hebrew texts on which they were based. Important in this introduction is a theory of local text types which has come to prominence since the discoveries at Qumran. The focus on the Septuagint in this book does not reflect an arbitrary selection of an aspect of the text critical endeavor for purposes of illustration, but is based on the author's conviction that the Greek versions in a great many instances provide an access to the earliest discernible stages in the history of the Old Testament text.

The importance of textual criticism cannot be doubted. Every reader of any translation of the Bible stands on the shoulders of this discipline, for translators must resolve—either poorly or well—questions concerning which text to translate. In one sense, translator and interpreter alike must always view textual criticism as their first and most basic step. *Which* text of a book, chapter, or verse will be translated? Which interpreted? The discipline speaks directly to the question, which words comprise the Bible. So textual criticism is not just another game which scholars play. It affects all who read that book, whether as an authoritative document of faith, as a mirror to self-understanding, or as a rich literary legacy from the ancient world.

GENE M. TUCKER

Emory University
Atlanta, Georgia
Spring, 1974

Contents

Preface

The conjunction *and* is typical of studies on the Septuagint (here-after: LXX), the Greek version of the Hebrew Bible. "The LXX *and* the New Testament" might be a study in the way New Testa-ment writers quoted this Bible translation, or it might indicate a philological analysis of LXX vocabulary or syntax in order to explain some feature of the New Testament. "The LXX *and* Helle-nistic Judaism" might be the name for an inquiry into how the theol-ogy of the first, somewhat Hellenized translators worked its way into the text, or how the LXX played an apologetic role for Jews in a Hellenistic world. "The LXX *and* the Early Church" might denote an investigation into the implications of the fact that many of the earliest church fathers used the LXX in preference to the Hebrew Bible. These implications might involve questions of canon, inspira-tion, or theological development in general.

However important these other studies on "the LXX *and*" might be, this book focuses particularly on the LXX and textual criticism. Textual criticism is the discipline that tries to recover the original copy (autograph) of a piece of literature by comparing its available copies, all of which inevitably contain mistakes. For the Hebrew Bible this task is complicated by the special factor that almost all early manuscripts have disappeared in whole or in part. The text printed in *Biblia Hebraica*, one of the most popular editions of the Hebrew Bible, is merely an unchanged reproduction of a manu-script from the eleventh century A.D. The few other manuscripts from approximately the same period show little variation from it. During more than a millennium of copying, however, hundreds of mistakes and changes must have crept into the text either by acci-dent or by intention. Since the extant earlier Hebrew evidence is either too fragmentary or already infected by scribal errors, scholars have long sought a way to recover earlier copies of the entire Bible. The LXX has provided one roundabout way to get to that earlier evidence. By translating the LXX back into Hebrew and then comparing this retroversion with whatever Hebrew manuscripts are available, text critics have managed to supplement the meager early Hebrew manuscripts.

This book concerns the LXX and textual criticism after Qumran. The discovery of the many ancient Hebrew and Greek fragments, popularly called the Dead Sea Scrolls, provided manuscripts one thousand years older than the manuscripts printed in *Biblia Hebraica*. Much of this evidence is contemporaneous with the Hebrew text scholars had reconstructed from the LXX. It affects our understanding of the LXX's use in textual criticism in at least two ways:

The scrolls have confirmed the idea that many departures from the Hebrew text in the LXX rest on real Hebrew variants rather than merely on the freedom allegedly exercised by the translators.

The Hebrew and Greek manuscripts from the Judean wilderness have enabled scholars to identify more precisely a series of recensions or revisions of the LXX, and they have led to the hypothesis that each geographical locale, such as Egypt or Palestine, had a Hebrew text type that was peculiar to it.

The scrolls, then, have brought new life to the old field of textual criticism. Not only do scholars have new manuscripts, many older than anything a previous generation dared hope for, but they also have new presuppositions and assumptions about utilizing the LXX for textual criticism. Suddenly, readings of the LXX which have been available for a long time take on new significance.

With this new life has also come controversy. Textual criticism has often been considered a "safe" discipline, in contrast to the methods of "higher criticism." The reader of this book will soon discover that in textual criticism, too, bold subjective decisions must sometimes be made and that leading scholars in the field will vigorously disagree with one another. In addition, textual criticism deals not only with trivial slips of ancient copyists, but it also involves major reworkings of biblical books, the interpretation of Hebrew manuscripts which have been considerably expanded or which are woefully full of lacunae, and new understandings of the editorial techniques employed by writers like the Chronicler, of the events in Israel's history, and of the chronology of the Old Testament. It helps clarify how the Bible was written and what is meant by inspiration. The issues, in short, are so important that the serious exegete cannot neglect them if he wants a valid understanding of the text.

This introduction to textual criticism is written for the college or seminary student who wants to chart a course through a complicated field. Recognizing that some students, who want to achieve a faithful understanding of the text, will not yet have mastered Greek and Hebrew, we have minimized the use of Greek and Hebrew words. If the point in question can be demonstrated by translating the Greek and Hebrew into English, that option will always be taken. Transliteration will be used only where absolutely necessary. This book is intended to introduce students to a new discipline. Continued experience with the LXX itself and wide reading in literature about it will come in due time. Hopefully, enough data is provided in this book that it can continue to serve the student as a convenient guide to the possibilities and problems of textual criticism long after he has passed the rank of "beginner."

Finally, the course herein charted is deeply influenced by my "doctor-father," Frank M. Cross, Jr., Hancock Professor of Hebrew and other Oriental Languages at Harvard University. His brilliant interpretations of the scrolls and their implications for LXX studies are at the heart of the proposals in this book. In addition, his encouragement during the "dog-days" of my doctoral dissertation and his enthusiasm for the results of that study, for the preparation of this book, and for a series of articles on text critical matters I have produced have frequently provided incentive to keep going and to persevere. If this book can serve to disseminate his insights for wider discussion and to equip students to share in the excitement of this "new-old" field, it will have met my goals for it and more.

RALPH W. KLEIN

St. Louis, Missouri
March, 1974

Glossary

AQUILA—A Jewish reviser of LXX whose style was extremely literalistic.

CAIRO GENIZA—A sealed storeroom of a synagogue in Old Cairo, discovered in the last century, which contained many Hebrew manuscripts, some dating back to the sixth century A.D.

CATENA—A commentary (literally "chains" of comments), compiled from writers such as the church fathers, Philo, or Josephus, which accompanies the biblical text in some LXX manuscripts. At times the ancient commentary is based on a different or older text than that given in the manuscript itself.

CONFLATION—The combination of two variant texts into one.

CURSIVES—The small letters, often joined together, in which Greek manuscripts were written from the ninth century on. Sometimes called minuscules.

DAUGHTER TRANSLATION—A translation of the LXX into another language, such as Latin, Ethiopic, Coptic, etc.

DITTOGRAPHY—A mistake in writing, when a copyist wrote twice what should have been written once.

GLOSSES—Extra words intended as explanations of the text. By accident or intention they were frequently inserted from the margin into the text itself.

HAPLOGRAPHY—A mistake in writing, when a copyist wrote once what should have been written twice; the opposite of dittography. Sometimes used to refer to any omission.

HEXAPLARIC—An adjective used to describe manuscripts which contain, in whole or in part, the additions inserted by Origen into the fifth column of the Hexapla.

HOMOEOARCHTON OR HOMOEOTELEUTON—An accidental omission by a copyist caused respectively by similar beginnings or similar endings on words. The copyist's eye skipped from the first to the second leaving out the intervening material.

ITACISM—The accidental confusion in Greek manuscripts of seven vowels or diphthongs which had a similar pronunciation.

JOSEPHUS—A Jewish historian whose citations from the Greek Bible are often from the proto-Lucianic recension.

KAIGE recension—A revision of the Greek text toward the MT, made in Palestine, shortly after the turn of the era. The name *kaige* comes from its peculiar translation of the Hebrew particle *gam* (also). Identical with proto-Theodotion.

LACUNA—A gap in an ancient manuscript where a portion of text has been destroyed.

LOCAL TEXT—A text form peculiar to a given locality, such as the Palestinian Hebrew text.

LXX—An abbreviation for the Septuagint.

LXX^L—An abbreviation for the Lucianic recension of LXX.

MASSORETES—Jewish scholars who added the vowel points to the Hebrew consonantal text in the sixth to ninth centuries A.D.

METATHESIS—A mistake in writing, when letters or words are given in an incorrect order.

MINUSCULES—See cursives.

MT—An abbreviation for Massoretic Text.

OLD GREEK—The original pre-Christian translation of the Bible, made in Egypt.

OLD LATIN—A second century A.D. daughter translation of LXX.

PROTO-LUCIAN—A revision of the Old Greek to agree with the Palestinian Hebrew text, in the second or first century B.C. In Samuel—Kings it can be recovered from manuscripts boc_2e_2.

PROTO-LXX—Another name for the Old Greek.

PROTO-THEODOTION—An early recension of the LXX, sometimes called the *kaige* recension, which was used by Theodotion as he made his further revision.

QUINTA—A fifth Greek column (in addition to Aquila, Symmachus, Theodotion, and LXX) used for some books in Origen's Hexapla. In the Minor Prophets, Quinta seems to be closely related to the *kaige* recension.

RECENSION—An edition of an ancient text, involving a revision of an earlier text form, e.g., the *kaige* recension.

RETROVERSION—A translation of the Greek text back into the Hebrew on which it was allegedly based.

SEPTIMA—A seventh Greek column (cf. Quinta) used for some books in Origen's Hexapla.

SEXTA—A sixth Greek column (cf. Quinta) used for some books in Origen's Hexapla.

SP—An abbreviation for the Samaritan Hebrew Pentateuch.

SYMMACHUS—A second-century A.D. reviser of the LXX.

SYNONYMOUS READINGS—Variants which result from the replacement of Hebrew words by others which are used interchangeably and synonymously with them elsewhere in the Old Testament.

SYRO-HEXAPLAR VERSION—A seventh-century Syriac translation of the fifth column of the Hexapla. It preserves the critical signs and marginal notes from Aquila, Symmachus, and Theodotion.

THEODOTION—A second-century Jewish reviser of the LXX who used the proto-Theodotionic recension as his base text.

TRANSLITERATION—The copying out of Hebrew letters in Greek script, instead of translating them. Common in Theodotion, but also employed elsewhere in LXX.

TRIFARIA VARIETAS—The three editions of the LXX (Hesychian, Hexaplaric, and Lucianic) referred to by Jerome in his preface to Chronicles.

UNCIAL—The modified form of capital letters in which Greek manuscripts were written from the fourth to the tenth centuries.

VORLAGE—The Hebrew text as it lay before the translator.

I

From Origin to Origen

The story of the Septuagint (LXX) begins with the translation of the Pentateuch in Alexandria, Egypt, in the third century B.C. Since the Jewish community there found increasing difficulty in using Hebrew, it translated the Pentateuch into *koine* Greek to meet the liturgical needs of the synagogue, and perhaps for apologetic and educational purposes as well. By the time of Christ, the complete Old Testament had been translated.

How do we know this? One source of information is the legendary Letter of Aristeas,[1] which asserts that the backer of the LXX project was none other than Ptolemy Philadelphus (285–247 B.C.). He wanted to collect all the books of the world and was informed by his librarian Demetrius that his collection should include a copy of the Jewish Law, which would have to be translated. The Egyptian king sent a delegation, including Aristeas, to Jerusalem to obtain from the High Priest Eleazar six elders from each of the twelve tribes who could accurately carry on the task of translation. The high priest gladly cooperated and sent with the translators a copy of the Hebrew Law written in letters of gold. To make a long story short, the elders finished their work in seventy-two days on the island of Pharos. After the results were compared and made to agree, the Jewish community accepted the translation with joy and expressed great concern that it never be altered. The king marveled at the Law and ordered vigilance and reverence in preserving it. Later, as this story was retold in the early church, it got "better and better." According to Justin Martyr, the translation included the whole Old Testament. Later in the second century Irenaeus reports that the translators worked in isolation but came up with identical

---

1. A translation is provided by Herbert T. Andrews in *Apocrypha and Pseudepigrapha of the Old Testament,* ed. Robert H. Charles (Oxford: At the Clarendon Press, 1913), II, pp. 83–122.

results, thanks to the inspiration of God. Finally, Epiphanius of Salamis (314–403) pushed the isolation idea to the limit. He had the translators do everything in pairs, even going by thirty-six boats each night to dine with the king. When the thirty-six independent translations were read before the king, they were found to be completely identical.

These traditions reported by Justin, Irenaeus, and Epiphanius are not reliable although they do reflect the great prestige the LXX enjoyed in early Christianity. But even the Letter of Aristeas is riddled with many historical improbabilities and errors. More than 250 years ago Humphrey Hody showed that the letter was not the work of a contemporary of Philadelphus, that is, it was not by the hand of a third-century Aristeas. What is more, Aristeas betrayed his Jewish faith in many incidental ways even though he tried to pass himself off as a devotee of Greek religion. Scholars have denied that Philadelphus commissioned the work and that remnants of the twelve tribes would still have been around from which to select the seventy-two elders. And yet, however legendary and improbable the details, many still believe that some accurate historical facts about the LXX can be distilled from Aristeas: (1) the translation began in the third century B.C.; (2) Egypt was the place of origin; and (3) the Pentateuch was done first.

To accept these facts while rejecting much of the rest of Aristeas as incredible requires other sources of information. The third-century date seems probable since a certain Demetrius (not Ptolemy's librarian!), writing at the end of the third century B.C., cites the book of Genesis according to the LXX's translation. Certain details of the Greek Pentateuch betray the language of early Ptolemaic Egypt or even of Alexandria itself. Thus, the author of the Letter of Aristeas is right in claiming that the translation was done in Egypt, but he errs when he narrates that the translators were recent immigrants from Palestine. Finally, stylistic comparisons have shown that the whole Bible was not done at one time. It is very probable that the Pentateuch was translated first because of its great authority and early "canonization" (perhaps at the time of Ezra) whereas the Prophets do not seem to have achieved canonical status before about 200 B.C., and the Writings may have retained the status of an open-ended collection for several more centuries.[2] The Prophets and perhaps even some of the Writings must have been translated by the

---

2. For documentation of this position and refutation of the notion of an Alexandrian canon, see Albert Sundberg, *The Old Testament of the Early Church* (Cambridge: Harvard University Press, 1964).

2

late second century, we believe, judging from the Prologue to the apocryphal book of Sirach (= Ecclesiasticus). Furthermore, a certain Eupolemus (cf. 1 Macc. 8:17) seems to have known the LXX of Chronicles in the second century B.C., and the book of 1 Maccabees quotes the Psalter according to LXX. All the Writings may not have been translated so early, but in the writings of Philo, the New Testament, and Josephus—all in the first century A.D.—references are made to nearly all the Old Testament books in their LXX dress. The translation of Ecclesiastes in the extant manuscripts, to be sure, is now ascribed to Aquila (ca. 130 A.D.), but this may have been a revision of an earlier translation.

Despite the many historical inaccuracies in the Letter of Aristeas, certain facts which it reports about the LXX have been confirmed then by other ancient sources. Surprisingly, this legendary letter continues to serve as a catalyst for all kinds of theories on LXX origins up to the present day, and these theories have serious implications for the history of the LXX and its proper use in textual criticism.

Aristeas played a role in the hypotheses of Paul Kahle (1875–1964) who seriously questioned the value of LXX in reconstructing an early form of the Hebrew text.[3] Kahle believed that there never was *an* original or proto-LXX, but that a number of partial translations were made to meet practical needs, just as seems to be the case with the Aramaic translations of the Bible, the Targums. He found support for this in the variety of ways the Greek Old Testament is cited in Philo, Josephus, the New Testament, and Justin Martyr. Kahle dated the Letter of Aristeas to about 130 B.C. (as do most others today) and argued that it was a propaganda piece for a recently revised translation of the Torah in the second half of the second century B.C. He interpreted the words "carelessly interpreted" in paragraph 30 of Aristeas to mean that a revision was necessary because the previous translations had been so carelessly made. In Kahle's opinion, even this revised translation is no longer extant. He claims that the canonical Christian Greek Old Testament, with which we are familiar, is a product of the second century of the Christian era or later. At most, therefore, the LXX could give us evidence for how the Hebrew Bible was read in the second Christian century. By that time, as we shall see, the period of major variations in the Hebrew text types seems to be over. If we follow Kahle, then the value of LXX for textual criticism of the Hebrew Bible is fairly minimal.

3. Paul Kahle, *The Cairo Geniza*, 2d ed. (Oxford: Basil Blackwell, 1959).

Recent years have seen the waning of Kahle's theories. While the technicalities of the critical argument can be avoided here, suffice it to say that his interpretation of the Greek citations in later Jewish and Christian writings has not been sustained. Even more damaging were the discovery and publication of a Greek translation of the Minor Prophets from the Nahal Hever in the wilderness of Judea. Far from showing the great variety of Greek translations in pre-Christian times, as Kahle at first proposed, this scroll is now seen as a revision of *the* LXX from about the turn of the era.[4] It lends impressive support to the idea that there was once a single original translation of the Bible, a proto-LXX.

What is more, Kahle seems to have been wrong about the intention of Aristeas. S. P. Brock has argued that the Letter of Aristeas was a defense of the Old Greek as is and a warning against any revision of it, not a propaganda piece for a revised translation.[5] Aristeas concedes to Palestinian critics of the LXX that the copies of the Hebrew Bible in third-century Alexandria were inaccurate or "carelessly interpretated" (paragraph 30), but thanks to the generosity of the high priest in Jerusalem, a special, authoritative copy of the Bible had been supplied to the original translators. Since Aristeas further relates that the high priest himself had supplied skilled translators from all twelve tribes, anyone who would impugn the LXX must impugn the high priest as well. The letter asserts that the original translation was of such high accuracy that no revision is necessary (paragraph 310), and it pronounces a curse on any who would seek to make changes in it (paragraph 311).

This hard-line approach in Aristeas may have been related to the discovery at his time of discrepancies between the Greek and Hebrew Bibles. Some of these discrepancies were caused by the fact that even the original LXX was not consistently literal. Others would have arisen subsequent to the translation of the LXX as the Hebrew text underwent various changes (additions, subtractions, copyists' errors, and the like). The number of such discrepancies would be multiplied many times if the LXX, based on the Hebrew text as transmitted in Egypt, were compared with the considerably different text types at home in places like Palestine or Babylon. Once discovered, such discrepancies could be dealt with in two ways. According to one, the difference would be labeled insignifi-

4. D. Barthélemy, *Les Devanciers d'Aquila,* VTS 10 (Leiden: E. J. Brill, 1963).
5. S. P. Brock, "The Phenomenon of the Septuagint," *OTS* 17 (1972): 11–36.

cant or irrelevant either because the Greek text was inspired or because the Hebrew text and the translators themselves were officially certified by the Jerusalem priesthood. Aristeas seems to point to such certification. But a second approach to discrepancies would be possible: the Greek could be changed to agree with the Hebrew text to which it was being compared. Brock believes that the warnings and curses recorded in Aristeas were meant to forestall this kind of revision.[6]

The type of early revision against which Aristeas was allegedly polemicizing can be found in the aforementioned Greek Minor Prophets scroll, dating to about the turn of the era. It consistently brings the Old Greek into close conformity with MT. Certain choices of vocabulary indicate that the revisers responsible for it may have also produced at the same time the Greek text of Daniel which has been usually ascribed to Theodotion, a second-century Jew from Ephesus.[7] In fact, it has long been known that the "Theodotionic" Greek of Daniel must have been produced earlier since Hebrews, Revelation, and the apocryphal 1 Baruch, all written in the first century A.D., already cite its translation rather than the Old Greek.[8] Another, even earlier, pre-Christian revision called proto-Lucian has also been isolated thanks to Josephus and to Hebrew copies of Samuel from Qumran (see below, especially Chapter II).

SECOND CENTURY REVISIONS

We can pass on now from the question of the origin of the Old Greek or proto-LXX to the well-known, second-century-A.D. revisions of Aquila, Symmachus, and Theodotion, called forth in part by the discrepancies between the Greek and Hebrew texts. Aquila's revision is perhaps the most easy to characterize since it is known for its extreme literalness and for its translation of Hebrew verbal

6. Sidney Jellicoe has a somewhat similar interpretation. In his view, the Letter of Aristeas is a polemic against an incipient rival translation and an apology for Jerusalem and its temple. See *The Septuagint and Modern Study* (Oxford: At the Clarendon Press, 1968), pp. 29–58.
7. Modern editions of Daniel LXX commonly print two texts: one is identified as the Old Greek, thought to have been translated in the late second or early first century B.C.; the other is ascribed to "Theodotion."
8. Numerous examples can be found in Henry Barclay Swete, *An Introduction to the Old Testament in Greek*, revised by R. R. Ottley (Cambridge: At the University Press, 1914), pp. 47–48. The latest discussion of the Theodotionic text of Daniel is that of Armin Schmitt, *Stammt der sogenannte "Θ"—Text bei Daniel wirklich von Theodotion?* (Göttingen: Vandenhoeck und Ruprecht, 1966).

roots in all their nominal and verbal derivatives by a single Greek stem. He also used the Greek adverb (so!) *syn* followed by the accusative case to represent *'et*, the (usually untranslated) sign of the definite accusative in Hebrew. D. Barthélemy has given extensive attention to the rules governing Aquila's revisions and has demonstrated that Aquila's revision was based on a prior revision of the original LXX, called the *kaige* recension.[9] Aquila seems to have been motivated in part by a desire to expunge certain readings in the LXX which were being used by Christians for apologetic purposes. A classic example is his use of a word meaning "young woman" instead of LXX's "virgin" in Isa. 7:14.[10] Aquila's translation has replaced the original LXX in our copies of Ecclesiastes while other excerpts survive in connected texts of Psalms and Kings from the Cairo Geniza, in marginal readings of certain codices, and in patristic citations.[11] Symmachus is not so well-known, and it is generally felt that his revision is of lesser value for the textual critic. His base text, too, may have been the *kaige* recension. He is known to have employed elegant Greek style and to have substituted idiomatic Greek renderings for wooden Hebrew constructions. Symmachus was used by Jerome as he prepared the Vulgate.

The third translator-reviser was Theodotion, a proselyte to Judaism thought to have lived in Ephesus. Transliteration instead of translation is one' of the hallmarks of Theodotion, a feature that extends even to well-known and frequent words. His consistent style can be described in great detail since rather lengthy excerpts of his work have survived.[12] Theodotion, too, seems to have utilized the *kaige* recension in his revision.

By the end of the second century A.D., therefore, at least the following Greek renditions were widely known in Christian circles: (1) the original LXX or Old Greek, (2) Aquila, (3) Symmachus, and (4) Theodotion.

9. Barthélemy, *Les Devanciers d' Aquila*, pp. 15–21, 32–33, and 81–88. The *kaige* recension was made about the turn of the era; it will be given extensive treatment in Chapter II. The Greek Minor Prophets scroll found in the Judean wilderness presents a text which belongs to the *kaige* recension.
10. In addition to Christian interpretations of genuine Old Greek readings, pro-Christian glosses were included in the LXX. Instead of the original Hebrew "Yahweh shall reign" in Ps. 96:10, some Greek texts apparently read "The Lord shall reign from a tree (= the cross)." The Greek is only preserved in a citation by Justin Martyr, but it is attested indirectly via the Old Latin.
11. Most of these are accessible in Joseph Reider's *An Index to Aquila*, completed and revised by Nigel Turner, VTS 12 (Leiden: E. J. Brill, 1966).
12. K. G. O'Connell, *The Theodotionic Revision of the Book of Exodus*, Harvard Semitic Monographs 3 (Cambridge: Harvard University Press, 1972).

6

ORIGEN'S HEXAPLA

A radical change in this situation was initiated by Origen (186–253/254). Space does not permit even a survey of all the achievements of this singular biblical scholar. His name is primarily important for LXX studies, however, because of his greatest work, the Hexapla. As is usual with Origen, this project has earned him both high praise and rather severe criticism.

First, the agreed-upon facts! Origen arranged the Hebrew and Greek texts at his disposal into a six-column Bible (230–245). In the first column, he recorded the Hebrew text of his day; in the second, the Hebrew in Greek transliteration; in the third, Aquila; in the fourth, Symmachus; in the fifth, the LXX; and in the sixth, Theodotion.[13] Whenever the LXX contained an expression that was not in the Hebrew Bible of his day, Origen marked that Greek reading with an obelus ($\div$) at the beginning and a metobelus (:) at the end. Whenever the LXX lacked an equivalent for a reading in the Hebrew Bible, he added such a Greek equivalent to his fifth column (usually taking it from Theodotion) and marked it with an asterisk ($\cdot \times \cdot$) at the beginning and a metobelus at the end. Thus one could read the fifth column with its notations and figure out how it compared with the Hebrew.[14]

Origen's intentions have been variously interpreted. According to many (e.g., Jellicoe, S. R. Driver), Origen was trying to restore the LXX to its original purity since he assumed the original LXX was that which agreed most closely with the Hebrew text as he knew it. We must ask, however, why Origen who considered the church's LXX to be the inspired Scripture would correct it by the Hebrew text of the Jews. That would seem to run counter to some of his basic theological attitudes. Professor Brock has proposed that Origen was not trying to reconstruct the original text of the LXX. Instead, he wrote the Hexapla as a tool for the Christian controversialist in his debates with the Jews.[15] Origen indicated those pas-

---

13. For some books, he had access to three additional Greek versions, and these fifth, sixth, and seventh Greek columns are called Quinta, Sexta, and Septima. The Septima, however, may never have been more than marginal notes. Occasionally, the columns did not contain what their title implied. Since the "LXX" of Ecclesiastes was really the work of Aquila, the translation in the Hexapla's third column cannot be by the same person. Many think that this column really contains Symmachus!

14. Origen, of course, made other changes and corrections in addition to those readings which only involved textual length.

15. S. P. Brock, "Origen's Aims as a Text Critic of the Old Testament," *TU* 107 (1970): 215–218.

sages which were additions in the LXX and lacking in the Hebrew Bible of his day (and therefore probably also lacking in Aquila, Symmachus, and Theodotion) lest the Jewish-Christian discussion get derailed on the question of whether the passage cited by the Christian disputant was really in the Bible or not. By the same token, Origen noted those passages which were in the Hebrew Bible of his day (and therefore probably attested in Aquila, Symmachus, and Theodotion) but not in the LXX since they might give additional arguments that could be used with some authority in Jewish-Christian debate. The comparison with Aquila, Symmachus, and Theodotion would be very important since the majority of Christian contacts were with Greek-speaking Jews. Thus Origen was trying to protect Christians against the charge that they had falsified the biblical texts. Brock's interpretation seems to square with Origen's own account in his famous Letter to Africanus.[16] In any case, Origen's text critical efforts were part of a larger program involving major theological controversy. This should alert every student of the Bible to the potential importance of the text critical task.

The history of the LXX was adversely affected by Origen's Hexapla since it tended to obliterate the most original and distinctive features of the Old Greek, led to the neglect of some genuine Old Greek manuscripts, and led to the insertion into others of many non-genuine readings. Various church fathers consulted the Hexapla before its destruction in the seventh century, but the entire Hexapla, running to almost 6,500 pages, was never copied. Instead, it became customary to copy only the fifth column.[17] Once removed from the Hexapla, however, the asterisks and obeli of this column would be meaningless—something like footnote numbers without footnotes. They were frequently omitted or the markings were confused one with the other. In time, they were totally omitted from most manuscripts, with disastrous results. While a shorter reading in the pre-Origenic LXX, for example, might help us discover where a gloss had been added to the Hebrew Bible, Origen's addition of a reading corresponding to the Hebrew in his fifth column had the effect—once his asterisk was lost—of canceling out the old evidence. Many LXX manuscripts we now have at our disposal offer a mixed text, dependent at least in part on his work. Such manuscripts are commonly called "hexaplaric," a pejorative term.

16. For a translation of Origen's letter, see *The Ante-Nicene Fathers,* ed. Alexander Roberts and James Donaldson (Grand Rapids: William B. Eerdmans, 1965), vol. 4, pp. 386–392.
17. A copy made by Pamphilius and Eusebius enjoyed wide circulation in the fourth century.

All is not lost, however. Some manuscripts, particularly the fourth-century codex Vaticanus (hereafter: B), seem to have largely escaped the revisions common to "hexaplaric" manuscripts. What is more, Syrian churchmen, among whom was Paul of Tella, translated the fifth column of the Hexapla into Syriac in the early seventh century. This "Syro Hexaplar," where preserved, is fairly accurate in recording the asterisks and obeli, so scholars can use it to reconstruct the pre-Origenic text. While the columns devoted to Aquila, Symmachus, and Theodotion have not survived completely, many of their readings can be recovered from the margins of LXX manuscripts and in patristic citations. These are available in a collection by F. Field[18] and in the apparatus to the Cambridge and Göttingen editions of LXX.[19] There remains one final factor to complicate this initial survey. Jerome (342–420) reported in his prologue to Chronicles that the Christian world had three different editions of the LXX (trifaria varietas). The Hexaplaric text of Origen was used in Palestine, an edition ascribed to Hesychius in Egypt, and a third ascribed to Lucian (martyred in 312) in Antioch of Syria. Little is known about the Hesychian recension. Some scholars doubt that it has survived; others are sharply divided on which manuscripts are Hesychian.[20] The text revised by Lucian, on the other hand, has been identified with reasonable certainty, at least for some books. Since the early Syrian church fathers Chrysostom (344–407) and Theodoret (386–457) frequently cited the Greek Bible, those manuscripts whose text agrees with their citations can be considered Lucianic.[21] It is often noted that Lucian filled in various kinds of omissions, preserved both readings (conflation) in cases where manuscripts had variants, replaced pronouns with proper nouns, and made various grammatical changes, including the replacement of Hellenistic with Attic forms.

Paul Anton de Lagarde (1827–1891) believed that if the Hesychian, Hexaplaric, and Lucianic recensions could be reconstructed from the extant manuscripts, the original would also be

18. Origenis Hexaplorum quae supersunt; sive veterum interpretum graecorum in totum vetus testamentum. 2 vols. (Oxford: At the Clarendon Press, 1867, 1874; reprint Hildesheim, 1964).
19. The Cambridge and Göttingen editions will be introduced in Chapter IV. D. Barthélemy plans a new collection of Hexaplaric readings.
20. See the survey of recent discussion in Jellicoe, The Septuagint and Modern Study, pp. 146–156. He believes that Codex Vaticanus preserves the Hesychian recension in many books.
21. See Bruce M. Metzger, "The Lucianic Recension of the Greek Bible," in Chapters in the History of New Testament Textual Criticism (Leiden: E. J. Brill, 1963), pp. 1–41.

within scholarly reach.[22] As it turns out, the history of the LXX is more complicated than Lagarde imagined, making the complete recovery of the original LXX a non-attainable goal. A case in point: the Lucianic text, though supposedly coming from the fourth century, seems to be closely related to the Greek Bible employed by Josephus at the end of the first Christian century, and it is already reflected in the second-century translation of the "LXX" called the Old Latin. These early or proto-Lucianic readings and the proto-Theodotionic recension (*kaige*) mentioned above are hints of the complexity of a full recovery of the LXX. Our knowledge of that history and our understanding of how to use the LXX in textual criticism has been radically advanced in the light shed by the discovery and interpretation of one of the greatest manuscript finds of all times: the Dead Sea Scrolls. In the next chapter we shall turn to that light.

22. See his *Septuaginta Studien* (Göttingen: Dieterichische Verlags-Buchhandlung, 1891).

II

The LXX and the Scrolls

The most widely used edition of the Hebrew Bible in America is Rudolf Kittel's *Biblia Hebraica* (BH[3]). Aside from some very minor matters, the text printed in this edition is a virtually unchanged reproduction of Codex Leningradensis from the eleventh century A.D.[1] At the bottom of each page are two apparatuses: the first contains variants of a more or less minor sort gleaned from other Hebrew manuscripts and especially the ancient versions (LXX, Samaritan Pentateuch, Syriac, Targum, and Vulgate); the second contains more important variants, again gathered from the same sources, plus a collection of proposals and emendations.[2]

Imagine how many times the Bible must have been copied between the time of the original autographs and this manuscript! Most scholars believe, for example, that the Deuteronomistic history (Deuteronomy, Joshua, Judges, 1–2 Samuel, and 1–2 Kings) was completed in the mid-sixth century B.C., the Pentateuch no later than 400 B.C. The manuscript printed in *Biblia Hebraica* was written more than 1,400 years later than either of these. We should expect to find that numerous variants were accidentally produced by copying the Bible over the ages, not to mention the possibility that intentional changes and supplements of considerable length may

1. This editorial procedure constrasts markedly with the principles employed in the Nestle-Aland edition of the New Testament. The text printed in Nestle-Aland is essentially the result of collating the nineteenth-century editions of Tischendorf, Westcott and Hort, and Weiss. While the Nestle-Aland text is not truly eclectic, nor does it always represent what the current editors think are the best readings (see the exclamation mark in the apparatus at 1 Pet. 3:18), it is surely much closer to that ideal than is *Biblia Hebraica*.

2. A new edition of this Bible, *Biblia Hebraica Stuttgartensia*, began to appear in 1968 under the editorship of Karl Elliger. Fascicles on Genesis, Numbers-Deuteronomy, Joshua-Judges, Isaiah, Jeremiah, Ezekiel, the Minor Prophets, and Psalms have already been published. New features include the evidence from the Dead Sea Scrolls, thousands of different interpretations, and the combination of the textual notes into one apparatus. The latter change is most appropriate since the previous assignment of variants to the major or minor apparatus was arbitrary and often wrong.

11

have been made in the course of more than a millennium of textual transmission.

Other medieval manuscripts of the Old Testament have long been known, although none of them is complete. The oldest dated Hebrew manuscript is a Cairo copy of the prophets from 895 A.D., while the Aleppo Codex, from about 930 A.D., carries the stamp of approval of the great philosopher Maimonides.[3] Other important manuscripts include a Babylonian Codex of the Prophets (916 A.D.) and a tenth-century copy of the Pentateuch in the British Museum. More than one thousand medieval manuscripts were examined for variants in the eighteenth century.[4] Despite variations in massora and other technical details, and even some variations in consonants and vowels, the text represented by these manuscripts does not differ dramatically from that printed in *Biblia Hebraica*.

Despite the relative lateness of Leningradensis and other manuscripts, a growing number of scholars have argued that these manuscripts do faithfully represent the text as it was in about the second century A.D. Some sort of normalization of the text seems to have occurred at that time under the leadership of Rabbi Akiba (ca. 50–135 A.D.). Paul de Lagarde believed that one master codex had been selected from which all subsequent copies have descended. Others have modified this hypothesis by saying that one recension (rather than a single manuscript) achieved preeminence in the second century, thus trying to account both for the consistency as well as for the minor variations that do occur in Hebrew manuscripts and in rabbinic citations. But even if it were possible to trace all medieval manuscripts back to one recension or one master text in the second century, we would still be extraordinarily far away from the presumed autographs.[5]

---

3. This manuscript forms the principal basis for the text of a new edition of the Hebrew Bible being published in Israel. During this manuscript's turbulent history, about one-fourth has been destroyed: Gen. 1:1–Deut. 28:17; parts of 2 Kings, Jeremiah; the Minor Prophets; 2 Chronicles; Ps. 15:1–25:2; Cant. 3:11 to the end; and all of Ecclesiastes, Lamentations, Esther, Daniel, Ezra, and Nehemiah. A series of four apparatuses in the Israeli edition will document all known variants from the Versions, Dead Sea Scrolls, rabbinic literature, and medieval manuscripts. See the sample pages in *The Book of Isaiah*, ed. M. H. Goshen-Gottstein (Jerusalem: Magnes Press, 1965).

4. See B. F. Kennicott, *Vetus Testamentum hebraicum cum variis lectionibus*, 2 vols. (Oxford, 1776–1780), and J. B. de Rossi. *Variae lectiones Veteris Testamenti*, 4 vols. and supp. in 2 (Parma, 1784–1798; reprinted Amsterdam: Philo Press, 1969–1970).

5. A splendid survey of these issues is given by Shemaryahu Talmon, "The Old Testament Text," in *The Cambridge History of the Bible, I; From the Beginnings to Jerome* (Cambridge: At the University Press, 1970), pp. 159–199.

EVIDENCE FOR AN EARLIER FORM OF THE HEBREW TEXT

Almost all Hebrew manuscripts written prior to the period of normalization have perished. To penetrate that textual vacuum, scholars have customarily turned to the earliest version of the Old Testament, the LXX. They believed that if the Greek text were translated back into Hebrew, they would have indirect evidence for reconstructing the Hebrew text of pre-Christian times. Several difficulties, however, bedevil this approach. First, it is not always possible to ascertain whether the divergences reconstructed on the basis of the LXX result from a divergence in the Hebrew text employed by the translators, or whether it is to be attributed to their paraphrastic style. Secondly, it has not been clear whether the divergences are merely a series of individual variants or whether different Hebrew text types existed before the MT emerged. Nowhere is this question posed more dramatically than in Jeremiah: does the LXX, which omits about one word of every eight, force us to conclude that there was once a radically shorter Hebrew text of Jeremiah, or is the brevity of the LXX the result of abbreviations made by the translator?

The discovery since 1947 of the Dead Sea Scrolls (250 B.C. to 68 A.D.) and other manuscripts from the Judean desert has moved this discussion to a new plateau.[6] In this chapter we shall examine a number of dramatic readings from these scrolls and sketch some of the new hypotheses that they have precipitated: (1) they have shown that many Septuagintal readings result in fact from Hebrew variants instead of free translation, and (2) they have helped sort out the revisions through which both Greek and Hebrew texts have passed. Obviously the brevity of our discussion, with its avoidance of many technical issues, can merely illustrate the argument rather than constitute its decisive proof.

We begin with a tiny Qumran fragment which illustrates, among other things, that certain LXX variations result from variations in a Hebrew text. Listed below are literal English versions of Exod. 1:1–6 in MT, LXX, and 4QEx^a (hereafter Qumran).[7]

---

6. The major finds are discussed by Patrick W. Skehan in "Texts and Versions," *Jerome Biblical Commentary*, ed. Raymond Brown, Joseph A. Fitzmeyer, and Roland Murphy (Englewood Cliffs. N.J.: Prentice-Hall, Inc., 1968), pp. 563–566. See also J. A. Sanders, "Palestinian Manuscripts 1947–1967," *JBL* 86 (1967): 431–440, and "Palestinian Manuscripts 1947–1972," *JJS* 24 (1973): 74–83.

7. This fragment was given provisional publication by Frank M. Cross, Jr., *The Ancient Library of Qumran* (Garden City, N.Y.: Doubleday and Company, 2d edition, 1961), pp. 184–186. The manuscript is dated to the Herodian period. Brackets in the Qumran text are reconstructions of lacunae. Cross discusses three possible variants in addition to the ones listed here. In one of them, the

MT: And these are the names of the sons of Israel who came to Egypt with Jacob—each and his household came: Reuben, Simeon, Levi and Judah, Issachar, Zebulun and Benjamin, Dan and Naphtali, Gad and Asher. And all the persons coming out of the loins of Jacob were seventy persons. And Joseph was in Egypt. And Joseph died.

LXX: These are the names of the sons of Israel who came to Egypt with Jacob, their father—each came with their household: Reuben, Simeon, Levi, Judah, Issachar, Zebulun, and Benjamin, Dan and Naphtali, Gad and Asher. And Joseph was in Egypt. And all the persons of Jacob were seventy-five [persons]. And Joseph died.

Qumran: [And these are the names of the sons of Israel who came to Egypt] with Jacob, their father—each [and his household came: Reuben, Simeon, Levi and Judah,] Issachar, Zebulun, Joseph and Benja[min, Dan and Naphtali, Gad and Asher. And all the persons of Jacob were] seventy-five persons. And Joseph [died.]

Despite the short length of this fragment, six important variants can be isolated:

A Unique Reading in Qumran

1. Joseph is included among those who went to Egypt with Jacob.

Qumran and LXX Agree against MT

2. Qumran and LXX add "their father" after Jacob; MT does not.
3. Qumran and LXX read "And all the persons of Jacob"; MT reads "And all the persons coming out of the loins of Jacob."
4. Qumran and LXX read "seventy-five"; MT reads "seventy."
5. Qumran and LXX read "persons. And Joseph died."; MT reads "persons. And Joseph was in Egypt. And Joseph died."

Qumran and MT Agree against LXX

6. Qumran and MT read: "Asher. And all the persons"; LXX reads "Asher. And Joseph was in Egypt. And all the persons."

How can these variants be explained? Each one must be examined in order before any general conclusions can be drawn.

The addition noted in number 2 is probably secondary since there is no obvious factor, such as a similar ending to the preceding word, which would explain why a copyist of MT would have omitted it, and since generally a shorter reading is to be preferred. The

---

Qumran fragment may agree with MT against LXX. When manuscripts like 4QEx* are cited, the "Q" stands for Qumran, the "4" for Cave 4 (there are 11 altogether), and the raised "a" indicates the first copy of Exodus identified from that cave.

Qumran fragment indicates that this supplement is not to be credited to the paraphrastic style in LXX; the LXX translators used an expanded Hebrew text divergent from MT.

The LXX's variation in number 3 again turns out to rest on a divergent Hebrew text. Which reading is original, the MT or the Hebrew used by the LXX translators and at Qumran? No final answer is possible. Both methods of indicating descent are in fact contained in the MT of Gen. 46:26.[8]

The variant "seventy-five" in number 4 is presupposed in Stephen's sermon (Acts 7:14) and is attested by some LXX manuscripts at Deut. 10:22. It is a secondary calculation based on a tradition like Gen. 46:20 LXX, where the names of five additional descendants of Ephraim and Manasseh have been added to the original text. Without these additional names, the MT's "seventy" is the correct total for the family of Jacob listed in Genesis 46.

The variants in numbers 1, 5, and 6 are clearly related, though distinct. The fact that the expression "And Joseph was in Egypt" is located in one place in LXX, in another place in MT, and in no place in Qumran is strong indication that it is secondary everywhere; in fact, it is likely that the text originally listed Joseph among the sons "who went down to Egypt with Jacob," as the Qumran document has it in reading number 1. A copyist, who was bothered by this apparent historical inaccuracy, deleted the word "Joseph" and replaced it with a marginal notation that Joseph was already in Egypt. When this corrected manuscript was later recopied by other scribes, the marginal notation was included at one place in the textual tradition behind MT and at a second place in the Hebrew tradition behind LXX.

Comparison of MT, LXX, and Qumran here has shown how the Qumran finds lend support to the thesis that divergences in LXX are often related to divergences in the Hebrew manuscript used by the translator. It also demonstrates that none of the three text types is necessarily superior; in each case possibilities and probabilities must be weighed. Finally, it is a good example of the subjective element in the decision-making process of textual criticism. Not everyone would accept our interpretation of numbers 1, 5, and 6.

---

8. Shemaryahu Talmon has labeled this type of variant "synonymous" and has published a series of articles explaining this phenomenon. "Double Readings in the Massoretic Text," *Textus* 1 (1960); 144–184; "Synonymous Readings in the Old Testament," *Scripta Hierosolymitana* 8: *Studies in the Bible,* ed. Chaim Rabin (Jerusalem: Magnes Press, 1961), pp. 335–383; and "Aspects of the Textual Transmission of the Bible in the Light of Qumran Manuscripts," *Textus* 4 (1964): 95–132.

THE SCROLLS, THE LXX, AND THE SAMARITAN PENTATEUCH

Another type of text found at Qumran has helped us to understand the Samaritan Pentateuch (SP) and how it is related to the LXX and the general history of the Hebrew text. The SP, preserved by the sectarian community whose home by New Testament times was in the vicinity of Shechem (cf. John 4), has about 6,000 variants when compared with MT, and it shares about 1,600 of these with the LXX. In our limited space we shall deal only with two types of these variants: sectarian readings and expansions.[9]

Sectarian readings. One of the principal tenets of the Samaritan sect was its belief that Shechem rather than Jerusalem was the only proper worship site. Through several devices the theological justification for this belief was inserted into their Pentateuch. Abraham's sacrifice of Isaac is transferred to Moreh (instead of MT's Moriah) near Shechem while the standard Deuteronomic cliché "the place which Yahweh will choose" is systematically emended to read "the place which Yahweh has chosen." This tense change transfers the Pentateuch's reference from God's choice of Jerusalem to his choice in patriarchal times of the city of Shechem. After Exod. 20:17 SP adds a command to build a sanctuary on Mt. Gerizim (cf. Deut. 11:29–30; 27:2–7). Likewise it makes Gerizim instead of Ebal the mount of blessing in Deut. 27:4. In recent years the Samaritan temple on Mt. Gerizim has been identified by archaeologists.

Expansions. These include various small additions (clarifications, insertions of personal names, etc.) and interpolations both large and small from parallel passages. So when Yahweh gives Moses a message for Pharaoh in the plague account, the SP frequently adds a passage which reports Moses' actual deliverance of the message (e.g., Exod. 7:18b SP, which repeats 7:16–18 MT). At another place (Exod. 14:12), the MT reports that the Israelites complained to Moses that they would have been better off if he had left them alone in Egypt instead of bringing them to the dangers of the Reed Sea, and then they ask, "Is not this what we said to you in Egypt?" According to MT, however, no such compaint had been voiced in Egypt. SP corrects this difficulty by adding the following words to

9. Bruce Waltke mentions the replacement of archaic forms, the removal of grammatical and historical difficulties, and scribal errors among other major variants. See his excellent survey, "The Samaritan Pentateuch and the Text of the Old Testament," in *New Perspectives on the Old Testament*, ed. J. Barton Payne (Waco, Tex.: Word Books, 1970), pp. 212–239. For the text of the Samaritan Pentateuch, see *Der Hebräische Pentateuch der Samaritaner*, ed. August Frieherrn von Gall (Giessen: Verlag von Alfred Töpelmann, 1918, reprint 1966).

the end of Exod. 6:9: "And they said to Moses, 'Let us alone and let us serve the Egyptians. For it would be better for us to serve the Egyptians than to die in the wilderness.'" Occasionally these expansions are reflected also in LXX. In Gen. 4:8 both LXX and SP supply Cain with the saying, "Let us go out into the field." Compare also the addition of "to the Hebrews" in Exod. 1:22 and "as a wife" in Exod. 2:21.

Several manuscripts from Qumran (e.g., 4QEx^f, 4QpaleoEx^m, 4QNum^b, and 4QTestimonies[10]) have greatly altered our understanding of these expansions. 4QEx^f, one of the oldest manuscripts from Qumran, adds the words "from their leaving Egypt" to the chronological notice in Exod. 40:17. Such a notice could have been taken from Exod. 16:1 and 19:1 where the MT also has it. What is more surprising, however, is that this same supplement to 40:17 is also attested in SP and LXX. In Exod. 32:10 MT, Yahweh tells Moses, "Now therefore let me alone, that my wrath may burn hot against them and I may consume them, but of you I will make a great nation." To this 4QpaleoEx^m adds: "and Yahweh was very angry with Aaron so as to be ready to destroy him, but Moses prayed on behalf of Aaron." The source of this supplement is Deut. 9:20, a parallel account of God's anger concerning the golden calf. The same supplement is found in SP. Similarly, 4QNum^b adds Deut. 3:23–24 after Num. 20:13, just as is done in the SP. While these and other Samaritan-type expansions have turned up at Qumran, the Qumran manuscripts do *not* contain the "sectarian" Samaritan readings.

These Qumran expansions have lent new significance to the fact that the LXX has about 1,600 readings in common with SP, and that Samaritan-type expansions also appear in the inter-testamental book of Jubilees.[11] What is more, when the writer of 1 Chronicles 1–9 cites data from the early chapters of Genesis, he too often cites "Samaritan" readings.[12] If the Jerusalem and Samaritan communi-

10. Frank M. Cross has explained the anomalous order of the passages in 4QTestimonies (Deut. 5:28–29; 18:18–19; Num. 24:15–17; Deut. 33:8–11; Psalms of Joshua) as resulting from an expansionist, Palestinian copy of the Pentateuch in which the passages from Deuteronomy had actually been inserted in the parallel context at Exod. 20:21. The passages in 4QTestimonies, therefore, follow the normal biblical order: Exodus, Numbers, Deuteronomy, Joshua. See "The Early History of the Qumran Community," *McCormick Quarterly* 21 (1968): 259–262.
11. Jubilees, LXX, and SP add the word "tower" to the text of Gen. 11:8 (Jub. 10:24) and the adjective "great" in Gen. 21:13 (Jub. 17:6).
12. Gillis Gerleman, *Synoptic Studies in the Old Testament* (Lund: C. W. K. Gleerup, 1948), p. 10. 1 Chr. 4:22, for example, spells a name as Cozeba whereas Gen. 38:5 MT has Chezib. The SP of Gen. 38:5 agrees with Chronicles!

ties broke totally about the time of Ezra and Nehemiah, as most handbooks to the Old Testament assert, why would a partisan of Jerusalem like the Chronicler, the rabidly orthodox writer of Jubilees, and the Essene monks at Qumran cite the Pentateuch according to the text of the separatist and sectarian community at Shechem?

To answer this question scholars have been forced to reevaluate the date of the Samaritan schism. They have proposed that the schism actually became total and final much later than usually proposed, perhaps early in the first century B.C., after the attacks on Shechem by John Hyrcanus. Up until that time the Samaritans used the same expansionist text of the Pentateuch that was employed by other Palestinians like the Chronicler, the author of Jubilees, and the copyists at Qumran.[13] This explains, in turn, why the Samaritan Hebrew script is related to the post-Maccabean, paleo-Hebrew script-revival at Qumran, why the use of vowel letters at Qumran and among the Samaritans is so similar, and why the Samaritan theology is influenced by late Jewish doctrines and practices: the split was not total until late.[14]

So the scrolls have helped to identify and limit the sectarian characteristics of SP to the references to Shechem and other specifically Samaritan theological comments. An expansionist text type of the Pentateuch itself was used throughout the Palestinian Jewish community until the emergence of MT. Such expansionist texts, as we shall see, are also characteristic of the Palestinian copies of Isaiah, Jeremiah, Ezekiel, and even Ezra.[15]

Incidentally, this approach helps modify a "rule" which has often been proposed, namely, that where LXX and SP agree against the MT, they are to be preferred. Since it was a copy of the Palestinian text which was taken to Egypt and was eventually used for the LXX, many agreements between LXX and SP reflect only a secondary reading in two closely related text families, whereas the original reading has been preserved in the isolated text family behind MT. According to the MT of Exod. 12:40, for example, the stay of the Israelites in Egypt lasted for 430 years. SP makes the 430 years

13. The Hebrew text used by the LXX translators is a branch of this Palestinian text; however, it assumed a separate history in Egypt no later than the fourth century.
14. Frank M. Cross, Jr., "Aspects of Samaritan and Jewish History in Late Persian and Hellenistic Times," *HTR* 59 (1966): 201–211; and James D. Purvis, *The Samaritan Pentateuch and the Origin of the Samaritan Sect* (Cambridge: Harvard University Press, 1966).
15. For the latter see the author's "Studies in the Greek Texts of the Chronicler" (Cambridge, Th.D. Dissertation, Harvard University, 1966).

cover the time Israel spent in the land of Canaan *and* in the land of Egypt; LXX reflects the same calculation although it includes the secondary "land of Canaan" at a different spot. Such variant word order, of course, is important evidence for the secondary character of the "land of Canaan." The MT chronology seems to be original.

THE SCROLLS AND THE EXPANSIONIST TEXT OF THE PROPHETS

The type of expansion just surveyed in the SP and in related Palestinian manuscripts of the Pentateuch was operative in the prophetic corpus as well. Sometimes the manuscripts from Qumran are expansionist. But we shall see that it is often the MT of the prophets that is the most expansionist. The shorter and more original form of the text has been preserved in the scrolls, the LXX, or both.

Isaiah

1QIs^a, containing almost all of the book of Isaiah, is the longest manuscript found at Qumran. Its text has much in common with the MT, and this has served both to demonstrate the arbitrary character of many emendations proposed by previous scholars and to show the great age of many suspect readings. This does not mean, however, that 1QIs^a or MT offers us the text in its earliest form. Rather, both 1QIs^a and MT are highly expansionist. Since the additions in 1QIs^a are not always the same as those in MT (or LXX), we can compare the two text types with one another in order to detect where supplements have been made in one of them. In the following examples, the words printed in italics are expansions found only in 1QIs^a; their source is probably the parallel passage from Isaiah cited in the parenthesis:[16]

1:15 Your hands are full of blood; *your fingers of iniquity* (59:3).

36:4 Say now to Hezekiah, *king of Judah* (37:10).

38:6 I will defend this city *for my own sake and for the sake of David my servant* (37:35).

51:3 Joy and gladness will be found in her, thanksgiving and the voice of song. *Sorrow and sighing will flee away.* (51:11).

60:13 The glory of Lebanon *he will give to you and it* will come to you (35:2).

16. The examples were compiled by Patrick W. Skehan in "The Qumran Manuscripts and Textual Criticism," VTS 4 (Leiden: E. J. Brill, 1957), p. 152. A related phenomenon can be seen in 34:4. There MT reads: "all the host of heaven shall rot away." 1QIs^a reads: "*and the valleys shall be cleft // and all the host of heaven shall fall* (like leaves)." The first colon is an expansion from Mic. 1:4; the second is a harmonization with a later clause in Isa. 34:4.

This evidence for expansion in a Hebrew text of Isaiah is instructive in studying the MT of such prophetic books as Jeremiah and Ezekiel, where shorter texts in Hebrew at Qumran or in the LXX lead to the judgment that the MT itself is highly expansionist.

Jeremiah

It is with Jeremiah that an expansionist hypothesis meets its acid test. The LXX of Jeremiah differs dramatically from MT, lacking one word in every eight, or about 2,700 words for the whole book. In addition, text critics have argued that the Oracles against Foreign Nations are secondary since the LXX contains them at a spot between what would be 25:13 and 25:15 in MT, whereas MT places these oracles, in a somewhat divergent order, at chapters 46–51.[17] Such variation in position is often the sign of textual expansion. In this case many scholars argue for the secondary character of these oracles also on literary critical grounds.

Modern scholars have long debated whether the LXX reflects a shorter and more original Hebrew text, or whether the translator has abbreviated the text. Many have adopted a mediating position. The scrolls have tipped the balance in the discussion since a passage has turned up which is short precisely where the LXX is short. This text, found in 4QJer[b], a Hasmonean manuscript, is a fragmentary excerpt from Jer. 10:4–11. At the corresponding spot in the LXX we find a translation for the equivalent of verses 4, 5a, 9, 5b, and 11 only— omitting verses 6–8 and 10. The Qumran fragment omits the same verses, but it cannot be determined how verse 5 was treated. The thirty-four letters of 4QJer[b] can be translated as follows:

[v. 4 . . . and with g] old men deck it; with hammers

[v. 4 is completed: v. 9 . . .] violet and purple

[v. 9 is completed: v. 11 . . .] shall perish from the earth.[18]

Though found in Palestine, 4QJer[b] represents the Egyptian form of the text, known heretofore primarily from the LXX. It gives at least partial victory to those who have argued that the short readings in LXX result from a shorter and more original *Hebrew* text. Preliminary reports also indicate that this fragmentary Qumran manuscript

17. I am heavily indebted in my understanding of the text of Jeremiah to J. Gerald Janzen whose Harvard dissertation has now been published as *Studies in the Text of Jeremiah* (Cambridge: Harvard University Press, 1973).
18. See the provisional publication by Cross, *The Ancient Library of Qumran*, p. 187, n. 38. Minor variations in the word order of the scroll do not affect our present discussion.

agrees elsewhere with the LXX in reading short names instead of the long names and epithets of MT.[19] As we shall see in detail in the next chapter, textual critics can use this new evidence as a base from which to approach the whole problem of the LXX in Jeremiah. Because of the extremely fragmentary nature of the Qumran manuscripts, most textual decisions still must be made on the basis of retroversion of the LXX into Hebrew.

QUMRAN AND THE TEXT OF SAMUEL

Scholars have long been aware of the great textual difficulties in the books of Samuel. Generally speaking, the most serious damage observable in the MT of Samuel is caused by haplography (=accidental omissions). Julius Wellhausen, S. R. Driver, and others were persuaded that the LXX often provided the best evidence for recovering a better form of the text. This hypothesis has been substantiated and considerably refined by the Qumran finds. Only a fraction of the Qumran data has been published, and many individual studies must still be completed, but two central facts seem established: (1) The LXX often does preserve a better text, and/or many of its departures from MT are the result of a different Hebrew text used by the translator, (2) Several different textual types are preserved in Greek manuscripts and each of them can be correlated with a corresponding Hebrew text type.

1. The superiority of LXX and/or its dependence on a non-Massoretic Hebrew text. The following examples are taken from the preliminary publication of 4QSam[b], one of the oldest manuscripts at Qumran, dating to the last quarter of the third century B.C.[20] They demonstrate that many variants in the LXX are in fact literal translations of a Hebrew text type different from MT. In addition, they suggest how valuable the LXX *alone* may be for those parts of Samuel for which there is no evidence from the scrolls.

4QSam[b] and LXX		MT
1 Sam. 16:2	Take a heifer along. (verb is imperative)	You shall take a heifer along. (verb is imperfect indicative)
1 Sam. 16:4	Is your visit peaceful, O seer?	Is your visit peaceful?

19. Another manuscript from Qumran, 4QJer[a], shows that the full, developed text of Jeremiah existed already about 200 B.C. in Palestine.
20. Frank M. Cross, Jr., "The Oldest Manuscripts from Qumran," *JBL* 74 (1955): 165–172.

1 Sam. 21:5	If the men have abstained from women, you may eat some of that (bread).	If the men have abstained from women
1 Sam. 21:6	All the young men have been consecrated.	The vessels of the young men have been consecrated.
1 Sam. 23:11	Tell your servant.	Please tell your servant.
1 Sam. 23:14	Yahweh did not deliver him.	God did not deliver him.
1 Sam. 23:16	in Yahweh	in God

2. *The variety of Greek texts in Samuel and their correlation with a variety of Hebrew texts.* The relationship between the Qumran manuscripts and LXX, which was detected in early studies, soon had to be modified and made more precise. Some Qumran readings could be correlated only with the Greek contained in the Lucianic family of manuscripts (LXX^L)[21] while the majority of LXX manuscripts, represented here by Codex Vaticanus (LXX^B), contained a translation of a Hebrew text identical with MT. Thus: 4QSam=LXX^L; MT=LXX^B. In the following list of readings, line (a) always contains MT and LXX^B; line (b) 4QSam and LXX^L.

1 Sam.	5:9	(a)	But after they had brought it (= the ark) around
		(b)	But after they had brought (it) around to Gath
1 Sam.	5:10	(a)	ark of God
		(b)	ark of the God of Israel
1 Sam.	23:13	(a)	And to Saul it was told that David had escaped.
		(b)	It was told to Saul that David had escaped.
2 Sam.	13:13	(a)	Jonadab
		(b)	Jonathan
2 Sam.	12:12	(a)	Yahweh
		(b)	Elohim
2 Sam.	24:17	(a)	I have done wickedly.
		(b)	I, the shepherd, have acted evilly.
2 Sam.	24:18	(a)	And he said to him . . .
		(b)	And he said . . .
2 Sam.	24:20	(a)	Expression lacking . . .
		(b)	And Ornan was threshing wheat [only in 4QSam^a and Josephus] . . .

21. These readings are discussed by Cross in "The History of the Biblical Text in the Light of Discoveries in the Judean Desert," *HTR* 57 (1964): 292–294. In Samuel and Kings the Lucianic text is contained in the cursive manuscripts boc₂e₂.

These readings must be evaluated in the light of two other factors. First, Lucianic readings occur occasionally in Josephus (first century A.D.) and the Old Latin translation (second century A.D.) even though the Lucianic revision supposedly came only in the fourth century A.D. This suggests that Lucian was dependent on an earlier revision, a proto-Lucian. Second, LXX^L shows enough agreement with the Old Greek to indicate that it is not a completely new translation, but only a revision of the Old Greek.

Qumran has supplied the missing links necessary for changing these observations into the following hypothesis: The Old Greek was revised in pre-Christian times to conform to a divergent Hebrew text type now known from Qumran. Since this revision formed the basis for the further editorial activities ascribed to the church father Lucian it is called the proto-Lucianic recension. Or, to state it differently: (1) The Old Greek was based on a Hebrew text in Egypt often superior to MT. (2) The proto-Lucianic recension is a revision of the Old Greek to bring it into line with Hebrew texts known from Palestine. (3) The Lucianic recension, while based on a Hebrew text much like MT, has as its substructure the proto-Lucianic recension.

Qumran and the LXX supply not only a variety of superior readings in Samuel; they also enable us to identify three distinct textual types. The implications of these conclusions will be amply illustrated in subsequent chapters when we use the LXX to study texts of Samuel for which Qumran readings have not been preserved.

THE KAIGE RECENSION

In 1952 Palestinian authorities purchased a collection of manuscripts which came from the Nahal Hever in the Judean wilderness, rather than from Qumran itself. Among these was a copy of the Minor Prophets in Greek, including portions of Jonah, Micah, Nahum, Habakkuk, Zephaniah, and Zechariah (possibly also Amos).

On the basis of preliminary publications of this scroll in 1953 and again in 1963,[22] five major observations can be made.

1. On the basis of paleographic evidence, the scroll (hereafter R) can be dated to the first half of the first century of the Christian era.

2. The Hebrew text type presupposed by R is related to, but is not so fully developed as MT. For this reason we designate it proto-

---

22. D. Barthélemy, "Redécouverte d'un chainon manquant de l'histoire de la Septante," *RB* 60 (1953): 18–29 and *Les Devanciers d'Aquila*, VTS 10 (Leiden: E. J. Brill, 1963).

Massoretic. In comparing LXX, R, and MT, Barthélemy found that R is usually closer to MT than the LXX is.

3. R is not a new translation, but it is a revision of the Old Greek.

4. R is characterized by unusual translation techniques. One of the more prominent of these is the rendition of the Hebrew particle *gam* (also) by the idiomatic *kaige*; hence R has come to be called part of the *kaige* recension. In addition, the word *'iš* (man) is consistently rendered by *anēr* (man) even when it has the distributive sense of "each." The Old Greek translated the latter cases with the word *hekastos* (each). Hebrew expressions are given a uniform rendition often at the expense of Greek usage and idiom.

5. R seems to be similar to or identical with Origen's Quinta. It is also reflected in biblical citations of the church father Justin Martyr (103?–165) and it lies behind certain readings in the Sahidic Coptic version and in the Greek Codex Washingtonensis.

Besides the obvious value these findings have for textual studies of the Minor Prophets, they also have revolutionized the approach to certain parts of other books. Barthélemy was able to show that this *kaige* recension is present in parts of Samuel-Kings, in the LXX of Lamentations, Ruth, and possibly Canticles, in the "B" manuscript family of Judges (the evidence here is not decisive), in the Theodotionic text of Daniel, the Theodotionic supplements to the LXX of Jeremiah and Job, and in the Quinta of the Psalter. (It probably also supplied the textual base for the revisions of Aquila, Symmachus, and Theodotion). In all these cases we see the same unusual translation techniques employed in such a consistent way that they must have been done by the same man, or at least by the same school.

Since the Theodotionic text of Daniel must now be identified as part of the *kaige* recension, it is clear how its "Theodotionic" readings can be cited in the New Testament and in other first-century works: these authors were merely using a revised Greek text of Daniel current already at their time. The characteristics of the real Theodotion of the second century, who must be distinguished from the *kaige* recensor, have been studied in detail by Kevin C. O'Connell on the basis of extensive Theodotionic readings in Exodus.[23]

As for Samuel-Kings, Henry St. John Thackeray had previously demonstrated that the translation preserved by the major uncial

23. *The Theodotionic Revision of the Book of Exodus* (Cambridge: Harvard University Press, 1972).

manuscripts was not uniform.[24] Sections *a* (1 Samuel), *bb* (2 Sam. 1:1–9:13), and *gg* (1 Kings 2:12–21) seem to be by one hand; sections *bg* (2 Sam. 10:1 to 1 Kings 2:11) and *gd* (1 Kings 22 and 2 Kings) by another. According to Thackeray, the earliest Alexandrian version of Samuel-Kings omitted sections *bg* and *gd* because they contained things derogatory to David and because they showed the growing degeneracy of the kings. He proposed that these sections were eventually translated by a Western Asiatic, an Ephesian Jew, who was a predecessor of Theodotion. This man has therefore been commonly called proto-Theodotion (Ur-Theodotion).

Barthélemy builds on this hypothesis and modifies it. He proposes that the "LXX" in *bg* and *gd* is not a new translation, but a revision of the old Alexandrian version.[25] The exact reason why only these two sections contain the *kaige* recension is not clear although Emanuel Tov has suggested that it may have resulted from the accidental mixing of scrolls of various text types (Old Greek and *kaige*).[26]

Thus, Qumran documents have led to a complex analysis of the Greek manuscripts of Samuel: some of them are Old Greek; some proto-Lucian as modified by Lucian himself; some *kaige*. Competent work on the LXX of Samuel-Kings can only be done at the hand of a critical edition like the Cambridge Septuagint, which lists the minuscules that contain the Lucianic evidence. The student has to identify carefully the character of the Greek text from section to section even within the major uncials, including Vaticanus. Perhaps the following chart will make this last point clear:[27]

Section of Samuel-Kings	Text Type in Major Greek Uncials
a	Old Greek
bb	Old Greek
bg	Kaige
gg	Old Greek
gd	Kaige

24. *The Septuagint and Jewish Worship* (London: Oxford University Press, 2d edition, 1923). Uncial manuscripts belong to the time between the fourth and tenth centuries; the word uncial refers to the large size of the letters. The limits assigned here to *bb* and *bg* were discovered by James Donald Shenkel.
25. Remnants of that older version can still be recovered from the Lucianic family of manuscripts.
26. "The State of the Question: Problems and Proposed Solutions," *1972 Proceedings of the International Organization for Septuagint and Cognate Studies* 2 (Missoula, Mont.: Society of Biblical Literature, 1972), p. 5.
27. The manuscripts boc$_2$e$_2$ in all sections of Samuel-Kings contain the Lucianic recension (in the strict sense), but proto-Lucianic readings can be recovered from them. A relatively pure form of proto-Lucian is contained in the readings designated by the symbol *theta* in section *bg;* in section *gd* the readings marked with a *theta* are from Theodotion.

In short, we have access via the Old Greek to the Hebrew text type preserved in Alexandria for sections *a, bb,* and *gg.* A revision, the *kaige* recension, made about the turn of the era, stands in sections *bg* and *gd.* The Hebrew text type presupposed in this revision was substantially the same as MT, but vastly different from that Hebrew text used by the translators of the Old Greek. The proto-Lucianic recension, which we discussed above, was also a revision of the Old Greek on the basis of the Hebrew. This revision was made in pre-Christian times, and presumably in Palestine, since the Hebrew text presupposed seems to be substantially identical with certain of the Samuel scrolls from Qumran.

Perhaps we should conclude this chapter by sketching what we believe to be the textual history of both the Hebrew and Greek texts in Samuel-Kings on the basis of the new evidence of the Dead Sea Scrolls.

Sometime after the composition of Samuel-Kings, and no earlier than the fourth century, a Hebrew copy of this work was taken to Egypt. Some variants no doubt subsequently arose in the local Egyptian text, in addition to those that had arisen during its Palestinian transmission.

A copy of this Hebrew text in Egypt was translated in the third or second century B.C. This is the Old Greek, and it is preserved in the major uncial manuscripts for sections *a, bb,* and *gg.*

The Hebrew text as transmitted in Palestine is evidenced by manuscripts from Qumran, and it accounts for some of the unique citations from Samuel-Kings in parallel passages of Chronicles, as we will demonstrate in the next chapter. In the second or early first century B.C., the Old Greek was revised to conform more closely to this Palestinian text. This revision is partially preserved in the Greek of Josephus and later formed the basis for the recension of Lucian.

A Greek text (Old Greek or proto-Lucian) was revised about the turn of the era on the basis of a significantly different Hebrew text type whose provenance may have been Babylon. This revision is known as the *kaige* recension and is preserved in sections *bg* and *gd* of the major manuscripts (cf. the text portion of the Cambridge LXX or Rahlfs). Various unique Greek equivalents were introduced.

After the final selection of the text type known as MT, the *kaige* recension underwent further development at the hands of Aquila, Symmachus, and Theodotion. Only fragments of these revisions have been preserved.

III

The LXX—It Does Make a Difference

Our survey of the Dead Sea Scrolls has shown that many variant readings of the LXX reflect a different Hebrew text, sometimes a superior one, sometimes merely one from a different Hebrew tradition. We have also seen that distinct Hebrew text types lie behind the Old Greek, proto-Lucian, *kaige*, and the Hexapla. We plan to move on in this chapter to readings where the Qumran data has not survived, but where the "LXX" itself, in its various recensions, is the primary evidence for variation. We shall examine the evidence for widespread haplography in the MT of 1 Samuel, for extensive expansion in the MT of Jeremiah, for variant chronologies during the textual history of 1 and 2 Kings, for an alternate historical reconstruction in 1 Kings 12, and even for new evaluations of the editor's sources and his theological bias in Chronicles.

HAPLOGRAPHY IN 1 SAMUEL

The copy of Samuel printed in our Hebrew Bibles is in a notoriously bad condition. The following selection of readings is only a representative sample of one kind of variation that is frequently encountered. Many of the emendations which we propose on the basis of the LXX have already been included in modern English translations such as RSV, NEB, and NAB, sometimes with a note informing the reader of the change, sometimes without such a note. A student should be aware of these notable variations as he tries to understand the transmission history of the Bible, and he should be alerted to the fact that there are dozens of such variations that are not included in modern translations, in modern critical commentaries, or even noted in the apparatus of *Biblia Hebraica*.

Since our selection of passages is from 1 Samuel, the LXX we will cite is basically the Old Greek. Even more complicated and sophisticated operations would be possible elsewhere in Samuel where the *kaige* recension is extant or where Qumran materials are available. To simplify matters we will pay little attention to proto-Lucianic readings. Our selection of examples, therefore, is arbitrary, intended only to illustrate the type of differences use of the LXX discloses. We have chosen readings which illustrate how Samuel MT is haplographic; that is, expressions original to the text have dropped out of all existing Hebrew manuscripts by accident. Words attested by both MT and LXX are printed in regular type while expressions contained only in the LXX are in italics.

1. 1 Sam. 3:15
   And Samuel slept until the morning, *and he got up in the morning,* and he opened the doors. . . .

2. 1 Sam. 4:1
   And the word of Samuel came to all Israel. *And in those days the Philistines gathered themselves for war against Israel,* and Israel went out to meet the Philistines [LXX: them] for war.

3. 1 Sam. 10:1
   Has not[1] *Yahweh anointed you as commander over his people, over Israel? And you shall govern the people of Yahweh and save them from the hand of their enemies round about. And this will be a sign to you that* Yahweh has anointed you to be a commander over his heritage. . . .

4. 1 Sam. 12:8
   When Jacob *and his sons* came to Egypt, *the Egyptians afflicted them,* and your fathers cried to Yahweh.

5. 1 Sam. 14:41
   MT: And Saul said to Yahweh God of Israel, "Give a perfect (lot)."
   LXX: And Saul said, "Yahweh God of Israel, *why did you not answer your servant today? If there is blame in me or in Jonathan my son, O Yahweh God of Israel, give Urim, but if it is in your people Israel,* give Thummim.

6. 1 Sam. 29:10
   And now get up in the morning, *you* and your lords' servants who come with you, *and go to the place which I picked out for you, and do not harbor a hostile idea in your heart (about my advice) for you are acceptable to me,* but get up in the morning, as soon as you have light, and go.[2]

It is interesting to see how these six readings are handled in representative modern English translations. The RSV only follows the

---

1. Hebrew *hălô*. A literal translation of MT would begin: "Is it not."
2. For an explanation of incidental difficulties in the above passages, see S. R. Driver, *Notes on the Hebrew Text and the Topography of the Books of Samuel* (Oxford: At the Clarendon Press, 1913), and Julius Wellhausen, *Der Text der Bücher Samuelis untersucht* (Göttingen: Vandenhoeck und Ruprect, 1871).

LXX in readings 3, 4, and 5, adding a brief footnote in each case. NEB follows the LXX in 2, 3, 4, 5, and 6, but it contains no footnote so that the average reader is unaware that he is reading an emended text.[3] Only the NAB follows the LXX in all six cases, but it too leaves the reader unadvised of these changes in most editions.[4]

In our opinion, the LXX's longer reading is superior and original in all six cases.[5] The reason for the defective MT in readings 1–5 is homoeoteleuton or homoeoarchton, that is, a scribe's eye skipped from one word to an identical word farther on, leaving out the intervening expression.[6] The omission in reading 6 was caused by simple carelessness—there are no obvious factors in the text that precipitated this mistake. Except for reading 1, the longer reading is essential if the passage is to make sense. In number 2, the longer LXX reading, which reports the assembling of the Philistine forces, explains why Israel went out to meet them. The reading preserved by the LXX in number 3 provides the *necessary* indication that the finding of the asses is to be a sign to Saul. Without "the Egyptians afflicted them" in reading 4, the verb "cried" would be most abrupt. In number 5, the Massoretes misunderstood the consonants *tmym* because of the haplography and pointed them as the adjective "perfect," instead of the noun "Thummim." The sentence as reconstructed on the basis of LXX makes clear that the Urim and Thummim were lots that were cast (cf. Deut. 33:8 and note "a" in BH[3]). The repetition of the words "get up in the morning" in the MT of reading 6 is seemingly unnecessary. But, with the inclusion of the longer reading preserved by the LXX, the reason for the double "get up in the morning" is clear.

Such haplographies can cause the omission of relatively long passages. All of the italicized material in the following passage from 2 Sam. 11:22–23 is supplied from the LXX and is probably original. As the text stands in MT (that is, without the addition) the terms in which the messenger speaks in verse 23 are unexplained. Homoeote-

---

3. Information on textual emendations has now been supplied in a separate publication. See L. H. Brockington, *The Hebrew Text of the Old Testament* (Cambridge: At the University Press, 1973).

4. Most editions of NAB omit this data. See *Textual Notes on the New American Bible* (Washington, D.C.: Catholic Biblical Association, 1973).

5. We refer only to the more major additions although "and his sons" in reading 4 and "you" in reading 6 may also be original. For the latter, see Driver, *Notes on the Hebrew Text*, p. 220.

6. Homoeoteleuton: reading 1 "morning ... morning"; reading 2 "Israel ... Israel"; reading 4 (in Hebrew) *"mṣrym wyʿnwn mṣrym"*; reading 5 "Israel ... Israel". Homoeoarchton: reading 3 (in Hebrew) *"Mšḥk yhwh ... ky mšḥk yhwh"*.

leuton (from "Joab" to "Joab")[7] and homoeoarchton (from "and he said" to "and he said")[7] caused the omission in MT.

2 Sam. 11:22–23: And the messenger went and came and told David all which Joab had instructed him, *all the words of war.* And David was angry with Joab. And he said to the messenger, "Why did you go so near the city to fight? Didn't you know that you would be struck down from the wall? Who killed Abimelech, son of Jerubbaal? Did not a woman throw on him an upper millstone from the wall and he died in Thebes? Why did you come near the wall?" (v. 23) And the messenger said to David, "The men had us at a disadvantage and they came out into the open field against us, but we pushed them back to the entrance of the gate."

EXPANSION IN THE MT OF JEREMIAH

Which text of Jeremiah is the more original, the longer MT or the shorter LXX? By using a short Qumran fragment (4QJer[b]) and the LXX, we demonstrated in Chapter II that preference should ordinarily be given to the shorter LXX. This observation can be illustrated and confirmed throughout the book of Jeremiah via the LXX alone. Since similar expansions are typical of fragments of the Pentateuch and Isaiah at Qumran and of the Palestinian Samaritan Pentateuch, it has been proposed that the expansionist MT of Jeremiah is a product of Palestinian reworking. We should note in passing that expansions could also be documented in Ezekiel MT via the LXX.

Conflation in Jeremiah MT

1. Jer. 25:6–7
   (a) *And do not provoke me to anger with the work of your hands. Then I will do you no harm.* (b) Yet you have not listened to me, says Yahweh, (c) that you might provoke me to anger with the work of your hands to your own harm.[8]

Synonymous variants arose in Hebrew manuscripts of Jeremiah, one (hypothetically) containing the sequence a-b, one (the Hebrew behind LXX) containing the sequence c-b. The LXX is thus both shorter than MT and divergent from its word order. Its divergent order, by the way, is important evidence that the LXX translator was not merely abbreviating. MT conflates the a-b and c-b text forms.

---

7. Following the Hebrew word order. The longer reading is included in NEB.
8. Italics in this section indicate what is in the MT, but lacking in LXX, whereas in our discussion of Samuel, they indicated what is in LXX, but lacking in MT. In both cases, italics are used to indicate material in the fuller text, not found in the shorter text.

2. Jer. 26:22
Then King Jehoiakim sent (a) men to Egypt, (b) *Elnathan son of Achbor and men with him to Egypt.*

LXX preserves the general information from alternate a while MT contains alongside this shorter reading the more detailed version of b. Interestingly, NEB omits expression a, contra LXX, presumably following BH[3]; the RSV equivocates by omitting, without comment, the second "to Egypt."

3. Jer. 41:10
Then Ishmael took captive (a) *all the rest of the people who were in Mizpah,/* the daughters of the king, (b) and all the people who were left in Mizpah/ whom Nebuzaradan, the captain of the guard, had committed to Gedaliah the son of Ahikam.

LXX translates expression b but locates it in the place occupied by a in MT—a itself is omitted in LXX. As in reading 1 above, the omission, combined with a divergent order, strongly suggests that a and b are synonymous variant readings conflated in MT. In this case, a may be original while b was produced by attraction to similar words in verse 16.

4. Jer. 42:2
Pray (a) *for us/* to Yahweh your God (b) for all this remnant.

LXX omits the italicized section a, and the Syriac omits section b. Clearly the MT conflates synonymous variants: "for us" and "for all this remnant."

5. Jer. 44:3
to burn incense, *to serve* other gods.

The Greek text represents only "to burn incense to other gods." We should probably reconstruct a hypothetical alternate Hebrew text reading only, "to serve other gods." MT again conflates.

6. Jer. 52:34
(a) Until the day of his death, (b) *all the days of his life.*

LXX omits expression b from this synonymous pair. 2 Kings 25:30, which is the basis for Jer. 52, omits expression a. Thus, alternate readings have been conflated in MT. (Cf. number 3.)

A special kind of conflation may lie behind some of the doublets in Jeremiah MT, especially where the LXX lacks one of two parallel passages. Commentators often remark that the LXX habitually omits doublets on their second occurrence, thus implying that the translator was jettisoning excess baggage. However, in the doublets 30:10–11//46:27–28 and 48:40b, 41b//49:22, LXX omits the *first* of the two readings. The doublet 6:13–15//8:10b–12 is most instructive. In this case, the second of the two passages is missing from LXX, but several considerations tend to negate the hypothesis that the Greek text is an abbreviation. J. Gerald Janzen noted two striking facts: (1) the orthography (spelling practices) in 6:13–15 is consistently fuller than 8:10b–12 and Jeremiah MT in general; and (2) 8:10a and 8:13 make the most sense if they were originally joined together without the intervening 8:10b–12. He proposed, therefore, that the reading was original in chapter 6, but was lost there due to homoeoteleuton (from "oracle of Yahweh" in 6:12 to "says Yahweh" in 6:15). Because of the similiarity of 6:12 to 8:10a, a corrector mistakenly reinserted the passage after 8:10a. Later, a manuscript containing the passage only in the secondary position in chapter 8 was corrected from a manuscript which still had the passage at its original place in chapter 6. By including the readings in both chapter 6 and chapter 8, a conflate text was formed (=MT). Fortunately, the variant orthography of the manuscript from which 6:13–15 was lifted demonstrates the probable correctness of this reconstruction.[9]

Expansion of Names

In expansionist texts the names of Yahweh or of human beings are frequently supplemented. Two examples of this are cited here. First, we include a statistical summary of the divine names used with the messenger formula "Thus says Yahweh."

	MT	LXX
1. Thus says Yahweh	85	119
2. Thus says Yahweh God of Israel	14	14
3. Thus says Yahweh of hosts	19	4
4. Thus says Yahweh of hosts the God of Israel	31	0
5. Thus says Yahweh the God of hosts	1	0
6. Thus says Yahweh the God of hosts the God of Israel	3	0
7. Thus says lord Yahweh	1	0
8. Thus says the Lord God	0	1

It will be noted that this messenger formula occurs some 154 times in MT, but only 138 times in the LXX, indicating sixteen probable

9. See J. Gerald Janzen, "Double Readings in the Text of Jeremiah," *HTR* 70 (1967): 444–445, for the technical data. The statistics for the following discussion of divine and proper names were taken from Janzen's dissertation, "Studies in the Text of Jeremiah." (Cambridge, Harvard University, 1965).

expansions. Even where both texts attest the formula the MT has frequently expanded the divine name. In items 3–7, for example, the MT has a longer divine name fifty-five times; the LXX, only four times. Another example is provided by the name "Johanan the son of Kareah." The man Johanan occurs fourteen times in chapters 40–43 always with his father's name, except for 41:15 where only the name Johanan is used. The LXX has the name thirteen times in the same contexts, but only four times does it have the patronymic. Significantly, it lacks the simple reference to Johanan in 41:15 as well. Judging by the expansionist tendency of MT noted above, we believe these ten shorter LXX readings reflect an unexpanded Hebrew base text.

One of the most convincing demonstrations that personal names were consistently added to MT involves the Babylonian king Nebuchadnezzar. In 27:6 to 29:3 MT this name occurs eight times, and each time it is lacking in the corresponding passage in LXX. The secondary character of these occurrences of the name Nebuchadnezzar is also suggested by the "n" in the fourth syllable. Normally, the books of Jeremiah and Ezekiel employ the philologically better form, Nebuchadrezzar. Whoever added the name Nebuchadnezzar spelled it in a way that is atypical for this book. His spelling habits lend support to our text critical judgment.

ADDITIONS FROM ELSEWHERE IN JEREMIAH

At times, the Hebrew text of Jeremiah was expanded by glosses drawn from parallel passages within the book itself. As we noted in Chapter II, such internal expansion is a regular feature of expansionist texts like the Samaritan Pentateuch and 1QIs[a]. The following three examples from Jeremiah illustrate this phenomenon.[10]

Jer. 27:1
In the beginning of the reign of Jehoiakim son of Josiah king of Judah, this word came to Jeremiah from Yahweh saying.

The information contained in this verse is, of course, incorrect since the confrontation with Hananiah which this chapter records took place during the reign of Zedekiah.[11]

---

10. These three examples and the three cited below under Deuteronomistic additions were published by Emanuel Tov, "L'incidence de la critique textuelle sur la critique littéraire dans le livre de Jérémie." *RB* 79 (1972): 189–199.
11. Three medieval Hebrew manuscripts, the Syriac, and Arabic read Zedekiah instead of Jehoiakim, but this is merely a secondary correction of an historical difficulty. Note the lateness of all three textual witnesses.

LXX's omission of the entire verse reflects a shorter and more original Hebrew text. The source of this addition to the MT is the identical verse at 26:1.

Jer. 28:14

For thus says Yahweh of hosts, the God of Israel: "I have put upon the neck of all these nations an iron yoke of servitude to *Nebuchadnezzar* the king of Babylon, *and they shall serve him, for I have given to him even the beasts of the field.*"

Again the LXX discloses the expansionist character of MT by omitting the italicized words. The source of these expansions may well be Jer. 27:6.

Jer. 46:14

Declare *in Egypt, and proclaim* in Migdol; and proclaim in Memphis *and Tahpanhes.*

The italicized words are absent from LXX. If we are correct in concluding that the shorter LXX text is also superior, the cause of this expansion may be a harmonization with 44:1 which relates that the Jews in Egypt lived at Migdol, at Tahpanhes, and at Memphis.

DEUTERONOMISTIC ADDITIONS IN JEREMIAH

The long sections of Jeremiah written in Deuteronomistic prose have vexed biblical scholars. Some argue that many of them are original; others that many of them are secondary. While the final solution to this problem lies well beyond the limits of this book, it can now be shown on the basis of the LXX that some of these passages came into the text during the process of textual transmission. Three examples will suffice.

Jer. 11:7–8

For I solemnly warned your fathers when I brought them out of the land of Egypt, warning them persistently, even to this day, saying, Obey my voice. Yet, they did not obey or incline their ear, but every one walked in the stubbornness of his evil heart. Therefore I brought upon them all the words of this covenant, which I commanded them to do, but they did not.

These verses are absent from the LXX in their entirety, and they bristle with Deuteronomistic terminology. Apparently a scribe steeped in this tradition composed these verses for insertion at this place.

34

Jer. 27:17–22

Do not listen to them; serve the king of Babylon and live. Should this city become a desolation? If they are prophets, and if the word of Yahweh is with them, then let them intercede with Yahweh [LXX: with me] *of hosts, that the vessels which are left in the house of Yahweh, in the house of the king of Judah, and in Jerusalem may go to Babylon.* For thus says Yahweh *of hosts concerning the pillars, the sea, the stands,* and the rest of vessels *which are left in this city, which Nebuchadnezzar the king of Babylon did not take away, when he took into exile from Jerusalem to Babylon Jeconiah the son of Jehoiakim, king of Judah, and all the nobles of Judah and Jerusalem—thus says Yahweh of hosts, the God of Israel, concerning the vessels which are left in the house of Yahweh, in the house of the king of Judah, and in Jerusalem*: They shall be carried to Babylon and *remain there until the day when I give attention to them,* says Yahweh. *Then I will bring them back and restore them to this place.*

The italicized portions are not attested in LXX (cf. also verses 13–14a). Some of the supplements in MT betray a Deuteronomistic hand; the rest result from a variety of other reasons.

Jer. 28:16

This very year you shall die, *because you have uttered rebellion against the Lord.*

If the italicized expression is supplementary, as the LXX seems to indicate, it may be drawn from a passage like Deut. 13:16.

This series of shorter readings from the LXX of Jeremiah suggests that it is absolutely essential to use the LXX not only for verse-by-verse exegesis, but also for investigating broader questions about the book's composition.[12] Since about 2,700 words of MT are absent from the LXX (nearly one-eighth of the total), the student must ask himself in every passage: What part of the text was already included in the final major redaction of the book, and what part of it arose during the course of textual transmission. It must be emphasized that the commentaries do not always note or correctly interpret the omissions witnessed by LXX. In Jeremiah, precise textual criticism must be performed if adequate historical critical exegesis is to be achieved.

---

12. The messianic passage 33:14–26, for example, seems to be a late insertion, updating 23:5–6. While the latter speaks of God raising a righteous branch for David, 33:14–26 calls Jerusalem a righteous branch and promises many successors for the Davidic king and the Levitic priests. Literary criticism indicates that 33 is from a much later writer who is trying to apply Jeremiah's words to the situation of post-exilic Jerusalem. In this case, the literary critical judgment is confirmed by the text critical data since 33:14–26 is absent from the LXX.

VARIANT CHRONOLOGIES

The mysterious and in part contradictory chronology in Kings has long intrigued scholars. Recently Edwin R. Thiele presented an ingenious solution to these problems based on two assumptions: (1) the figures in MT are original; and (2) a number of kings served coregencies with their fathers. By this latter proposal Thiele sought to explain why it is reported of the North Israelite king Joram, for example, that he began to reign in the second year of Jehoram (2 Kings 1:17) *and* in the eighteenth year of Jehoram's father Jehoshaphat (2 Kings 3:1), both of Judah. According to Thiele, Jehoram and Jehoshaphat had a period of coregency in which Jehoram's second year and Jehoshaphat's eighteenth would be identical.[13] Unfortunately, the Bible makes no mention of this and the many other coregencies which Thiele reconstructs, and his restriction of evidence to the MT appears unacceptable in view of our new knowledge of the history of the Hebrew and Greek texts. While a completely accurate absolute chronology cannot yet be reconstructed, enough research has been done to show that the Old Greek represents a Hebrew chronology that may be older than MT, and that understanding this textual history removes the need to manufacture coregencies.

As a case in point, we will outline the chronological evidence for a brief period of the divided monarchy on the basis of the data in MT and the Old Greek. This reconstruction is part of a larger hypothesis worked out in a dissertation by James Donald Shenkel.[14] Shenkel showed that no major chronological shift from the Old Greek was made in the proto-Lucianic recension, with the result that this recension can be used throughout the books of Kings as evidence for the Old Greek. This is helpful since the Old Greek is preserved in our extant manuscripts only through 1 Kings 21. For 1 Kings 22 and throughout 2 Kings most manuscripts contain the *kaige* recension whose chronology is the same as that presupposed in MT. As the tables below show, the Bible contains two types of chronological information: the number of a king's regnal years and a synchronism between this inauguration and the contemporary ruler in the other kingdom.

---

13. Edwin R. Thiele, *The Mysterious Numbers of the Hebrew Kings* (Grand Rapids: William B. Eerdmans, 1965), pp. 69–71.
14. Now published as *Chronology and Recensional Development in the Greek Text of Kings* (Cambridge: Harvard University Press, 1968).

Table A—MT's Chronology

Kings of Judah	Regnal Years	Synchronism	Biblical Ref.
Jehoshaphat	25	4th of Ahab	1 Kings 22:41
Jehoram	8	5th of Joram	2 Kings 8:16
Ahaziah	1	12th of Joram	2 Kings 8:25
Kings of Israel			
Omri	12	27th of Asa	1 Kings 16:15–16, 23
Ahab	22	38th of Asa	1 Kings 16:29
Ahaziah	2	17th of Jehoshaphat	1 Kings 22:52
Joram	12	18th of Jehoshaphat	2 Kings 3:1

Notes to Table A: MT contains another synchronism for Joram at 2 Kings 1:17—2nd of Jehoram. This synchronism represents a very late addition to the Hebrew text since it is attested neither in the major Greek manuscripts nor the (proto) Lucianic recension, but only in two late hexaplaric manuscripts (x, y).

Table B—Old Greek Chronology

Kings of Judah	Regnal Years	Synchronism	Biblical Ref.
Jehoshaphat	25	11th of Omri	1 Kings 16:28[a]15
Jehoram	11	2nd of Ahaziah	2 Kings 8:16
Ahaziah	1	11th of Joram	2 Kings 8:25
Kings of Israel			
Omri	12	31st of Asa	1 Kings 16:23
Ahab	22	2nd of Jehoshaphat	1 Kings 16:29
Ahaziah	2	24th of Jehoshaphat	1 Kings 22:52
Joram	12	2nd of Jehoram	2 Kings 1:18[a]

Notes to Table B: Shenkel reconstructed the chronological information for Jehoram on the basis of the internal evidence of the Old Greek chronology. In the Lucianic texts, the figures for Jehoram's regnal years and his synchronism with the kings of Israel have been corrected to MT.

For our purposes the most significant difference between these two chronologies is the alternate list of three contemporaries produced for Jehoshaphat. According to MT, Ahab, Ahaziah, and Joram ruled in Jehoshaphat's days in North Israel; in the Old Greek, the contemporary Northern kings were Omri, Ahab, and Ahaziah. Both systems, therefore, agree that Ahab and Ahaziah were Jehoshaphat's contemporaries, but the Old Greek makes Omri the third contemporary while MT gives that distinction to Joram.

15. A raised letter indicates additional verse(s) contained in the Greek but not in any extant Hebrew text. In this way the verse numbers in Hebrew and Greek remain synchronized.

What caused the change from the presumably more ancient Old Greek system to the data contained in MT? The answer may lie in a fresh examination of the battle reported in 2 Kings 3. According to MT, a coalition composed of Jehoshaphat of Judah, Joram of North Israel, and the king of Edom made war on the Moabites. During this adventure the prophet Elisha predicted a victory over the Moabites.

It has long been noticed that in the prophetic stories of Elisha (2 Kings 2–9), the kings of Israel and Judah tend to be anonymous. A perusal of the following tables will indicate that in an earlier state of the text this may have been true also with regard to this battle.

Table C—References to the King of Israel in 2 Kings 3:6–14

Verse	MT—B	Lucianic Manuscripts
6	the king Joram	Joram king of Israel
7	—	Joram
8	—	Joram
9	king of Israel	Joram king of Israel
10	king of Israel	king of Israel
11	king of Israel	king of Israel
12	king of Israel	king of Israel
13	king of Israel	king of Israel
14	king of Israel	king of Israel

While the Lucianic manuscripts have seven references to the Northern king and mention him four times by name, the corresponding references in the MT are all anonymous except for the first. The variety of expression between MT and LXX^L in this case suggests that the name Joram is secondary here as well. As Shenkel demonstrates convincingly, the name Joram in Lucian is accurate historically, but secondary textually.[16]

Table D—References to the King of Judah in 2 Kings 3:6–14

Verse	MT—B	Lucianic Manuscripts
7	Jehoshaphat king of Judah	Ahaziah king of Judah
7	—	Ahaziah
9	king of Judah	Ahaziah king of Judah
11	Jehoshaphat	king of Judah
12	Jehoshaphat	king of Judah
12	Jehoshaphat (LXX^B adds "king of Judah")	king of Judah
14	Jehoshaphat king of Judah	king of Judah

16. Shenkel, *Chronology and Recensional Development in the Greek Text of Kings,* p. 99.

Four of the five references to Jehoshaphat in MT are matched by references to an anonymous king of Judah in the Lucianic texts. In the fifth case, verse 7, the Lucianic manuscripts are directly contradictory, naming Ahaziah as king of Judah and repeating that information later in the same verse and in verse 9. The best solution to this confusion is to propose that originally all the references to the king of Judah were anonymous, and that they have been filled out in LXX[L] and MT in two quite different ways.

If Joram is the Northern king, the only candidates for the king of Judah acceptable according to the Old Greek chronology would be Jehoram or his successor Ahaziah. The references to Ahaziah in LXX[L] may be correct historical identifications even though they are secondary from a text critical perspective, or they may be mistaken identifications based on the parallel battle reported in 2 Kings 8:25–29.[17] In any case, the king of Judah cannot be Jehoshaphat since he was a contemporary with Omri, Ahab, and Ahaziah of North Israel, but not with Joram.

This conclusion is confirmed by a letter from Elijah to Jehoshaphat's son Jehoram recorded in 2 Chr. 21:12–15. While many hold this letter to be fictional, the Chronicler was clearly operating according to a chronology of the books of Kings which placed Elijah's translation into heaven and the beginning of Elisha's ministry *after* the death of Jehoshaphat. This chronology is preserved for us now only in the Old Greek of Kings but it must also have been the chronology of the Hebrew copy of Kings used by the Chronicler! Such a chronology would make it impossible for Jehoshaphat to appear in a prophetic story about Elisha, e.g., 2 Kings 3. Finally, we learn from 1 Kings 22:48f and 2 Kings 8:20 that there was no king in Edom during the reign of Jehoshaphat. Since the king of Edom is explicitly mentioned in 2 Kings 3, MT's identification of the originally anonymous "king of Judah" as Jehoshaphat is again shown to be errant.

Why, then, was Jehoshaphat inserted in MT? Part of the stimulus may have come from the parallel battle account in 1 Kings 22 where the circumstances and the vocabulary are so similar that they could easily lead to this faulty identification. In addition, later scribes may have been loath to have Elisha intercede for the likes of such Judeans as Ahaziah or Jehoram since Elisha had refused to heed

17. J. Maxwell Miller, "The Elisha Cycle and the Accounts of the Omride Wars," *JBL* 85 (1966): 441–454. See also Miller's dissertation, "The Omride Dynasty in the Light of Recent Literary Critical and Archeological Results" (Atlanta, Emory University, 1964).

Joram, the Northern king, because of his wickedness (2 Kings 6–7). According to any standards, Ahaziah and Jehoram of the South were not much better. Consequently, a scribe might feel that Jehoshaphat must have been the king of Judah involved.

To facilitate the match-up of Joram of North Israel and Jehoshaphat of Judah, who were not contemporaries according to the Old Greek chronology, a shift in chronological schemes was required. By beginning Omri's reign from the death of Zimri, rather than four years later after the death of Tibni, as in the Old Greek (cf. 1 Kings 16:22 LXX), the scribe made Joram's reign overlap with that of Jehoshaphat.

To get the full picture, we must fully evaluate the chronology in MT and Old Greek (Shenkel's book is indispensable). This sample reconstruction should suffice to indicate how valuable sophisticated use of the LXX is even for the student of Israelite chronology.[18]

JEROBOAM'S RISE TO POWER

In rare cases our reconstruction of the events of Israel's history may be significantly altered because of the textual data available through the LXX. The textual scholar must exercise caution in such cases and be ready to recognize the tentative nature of such reconstructions. The following example, nevertheless, illustrates the implications for historical reconstruction that the LXX can offer.[19] After the death of Solomon, a split between the Northern and Southern kingdoms ensued (1 Kings 12). Solomon's son and heir-apparent Rehoboam went to Shechem, the city where Joshua had forged his famous covenant (Joshua 24), to meet with a group of Northern dissidents who protested the oppressive service imposed by Solomon. Rehoboam rejected the conciliatory advice of his elders and decided on a tough line promulgated by a young group of hotheads. He sent Adoram, the head of the forced-labor battalions, to enforce his will, but this agent was summarily executed by the rebels. After Rehoboam had fled to Jerusalem, the Shechem assembly heard that Jero-

18. At a meeting of the Society of Biblical Literature in November, 1973, I presented a reconstruction of the chronology of Genesis 5 and 11 on the basis of MT, SP, and LXX. My essay demonstrated what the original chronological scheme was in both chapters, how that scheme has been modified in MT and/or the versions, and how individual readings within a given scheme arose. It will be published in a forthcoming issue of the *Harvard Theological Review*.
19. A more technical presentation of this reconstruction can be found in my article "Jeroboam's Rise to Power," *JBL* 89 (1970): 217–218. Serious criticisms to my presentation were raised by D. W. Gooding, "Jeroboam's Rise to Power: A Rejoinder," *JBL* 91 (1972): 529–533. My reply to Gooding is entitled "Once More: Jeroboam's Rise to Power," *JBL* 92 (1973): 582–584.

boam had returned from Egypt, where he had fled from Solomon. They invited him to Shechem and made him king. Although the action reflects Israel's abhorrence of the excesses of kingship, the division into two kingdoms was also facilitated by earlier separatist tendencies which David and Solomon were never able to put down completely.[20] One person's role remains quite ambiguous in all this—the new Northern king Jeroboam. He had received prophetic designation by Ahijah the Shilonite (1 Kings 11), an honor that had earned him the undying enmity of Solomon. According to the MT, Jeroboam joined all Israel in their demands for leniency (1 Kings 12:2–3a), and he was present with all the people when Rehoboam reported back his hard line (1 Kings 12:12). Strangely enough, however, 1 Kings 12:20 MT reports that it was only *after* the assassination of Adoram and the flight of Rehoboam that all Israel heard of his return from exile and enlisted him as king. For Jeroboam to have remained discreetly absent during the initial confrontation and the murder of the king's representative would have been valuable politically, but this convenient absence seems to be contradicted by references in verses 2–3a and 12 which assert his presence. Textual study resolves the contradiction.

Verse 12 of MT reports that "Jeroboam and all the people" came to Rehoboam on the third day after the Southern king had consulted with his two sets of advisors. But the LXX indicates that it was only "all Israel" who came to hear Rehoboam's decision. Although many textual critics have suggested that "Jeroboam" be deleted from MT, their case could be made stronger since the reading in the LXX is not only shorter, but actually divergent: it says "all Israel" rather than "Jeroboam and all the people."

Surprisingly enough, verses 2–3a are not even included in the Greek at their proper place.[21] If we conclude from this that an earlier form of the Hebrew text lacked these verses, in addition to the reference to Jeroboam in verse 12, then the whole chapter would be

---

20. David himself had first been crowned king in Hebron. Seven years later he received the allegiance of the Northern tribes (2 Sam. 5:5). Jerusalem—the "city of David"—and many parts of the ideal promised land first came under Israelite control through David. The revolts of Absalom and the subsequent anxiety of Northern elements under Sheba testify to an uneasy peace. A classic study of the United Monarchy as a union formed in the person of David was presented by Albrecht Alt, "The Formation of the Israelite State in Palestine," in *Essays on Old Testament History and Religion*, trans. R. A. Wilson (Garden City, N.Y.: Doubleday and Company, 1968), pp. 225–309.

21. A later hand added the equivalent of verse 2 to the LXX, but the insertion was made after 11:43. This secondary misplacement required the doubling of the regnal formula at that place, and it necessitated the creation of a substitute for verse 3a.

perfectly consistent. The people at first negotiated with Rehoboam while Jeroboam was still in exile. Only after the negotiations had broken down and violence against Adoram had been perpetrated did Jeroboam return and accept the invitation to kingship in what came to be known as the Northern Kingdom. This form of the text is plausible and displays political expedience on Jeroboam's part. If Jeroboam was exonerated in the original form of the text, why was it changed? A survey of chapter 12 in Hebrew and Greek indicates that verse 17 is present in Kings MT, and in the MT and LXX of 2 Chronicles 10, but is lacking in Kings LXX. This might indicate that this reference to Rehoboam ruling in the cities of Judah was borrowed by a scribe from the parallel account in Chronicles. The Chronicler's account may also have supplied the material hostile to Jeroboam which became verses 2–3a in 1 Kings 12. It is well-known that the Chronicler had a strong antipathy to the Northern kings, omitting most references to them or considerably disparaging their reputations. It would be typical of him to have Jeroboam participate in person in the rebellion from the very start. An additional textual observation may confirm this hypothesis. The subject of the sentence in 1 Kings 12:3a is "all the assembly of Israel." In Chronicles, on the other hand, the MT has "all Israel" whereas LXX[B] has "all the assembly." Thus the reading in Kings, "all the assembly of Israel," is a conflation of synonymous variants which are still separately attested in texts of Chronicles. This would indicate that the verse was supplied from Chronicles in a conflated and therefore late form, making the secondary character of 1 Kings 12:3a—which is, after all, lacking in LXX—reasonably certain.

NEW VIEWS ON REDACTION

Textual criticism also affects our understanding of the composition and redaction of biblical books. The book of Jeremiah, as we have already seen, was extensively expanded, even during the transmission process that followed the basic redaction. Another interesting study in redaction criticism can be made in the books of Chronicles, composed in the fourth century B.C., where the author used the earlier books of Samuel-Kings as his principal sources.[22] While he omitted many items (David's adultery, Absalom's rebellion, and almost all data dealing with the Northern Kingdom), he also added a good deal of new information and many comments of his own.

22. The Chronicler also refers to the book of the Kings of Israel and Judah, the royal book of Judah and Israel, the Acts of the Kings of Israel, the Acts of Nathan the Prophet, etc.

Great interest, however, has centered on how he cited the synoptic material from his Samuel-Kings source. Certain changes in content have been attributed to theological bias while others of a more minor sort have been identified as the result of inexact quotation or paraphrase. Lying behind many of these conclusions is the assumption that the text of Samuel-Kings employed by the Chronicler was virtually identical with our present MT. Impressive divergences have thus been discovered.

But are all these deviations to be attributed to the Chronicler and his alleged theological or political biases? We have seen that the MT of Samuel is highly corrupt. What if the Chronicler used a superior text? We have also seen that the Qumran copies of Samuel, the citations in Josephus, and the Hebrew texts presupposed by the LXX in its Old Greek, proto-Lucianic, and *kaige* forms have led to the tentative identification of three local text types of Samuel-Kings, which can be assigned to Egypt, Palestine, and Babylon respectively. Since the Chronicler clearly wrote in Palestine, the only way to evaluate his editorial principles is to compare his text with the Palestinian text of Samuel-Kings insofar as it can be reconstructed from our fragmentary Greek and Hebrew sources. To illustrate the difference this makes, we shall examine certain passages in which the Chronicler's bias has been detected solely on the basis of comparisons of our present Hebrew texts. When the Chronicler's sources are examined in their Palestinian form, many of these biases disappear.[23]

1 Chr. 14:12
And they [the Philistines] had left their gods there, and David gave orders and they burned them with fire.

2 Sam. 5:21
And they [the Philistines] had left their idols there, and his men carried them away.

Some scholars have interpreted David's orders to burn the gods with fire as an intentional change by the Chronicler designed to picture David as conforming perfectly with the Torah: "The graven images of their gods you shall burn with fire." (Deut. 7:25) The Lucianic family of LXX manuscripts in Samuel, however, preserves an additional clause which may be translated: "And David commanded to

23. This new understanding was worked out in detail by Werner E. Lemke in his dissertation, "Synoptic Studies in the Chronicler's History" (Cambridge, Harvard University, 1964). The specific examples which follow are drawn from this dissertation and from an article by Lemke, "The Synoptic Problem in the Chronicler's History," *HTR* 58 (1965): 349–363.

burn them in fire." We can conclude that this Greek is a translation of a variant Hebrew text of Samuel and that this alternate Hebrew text was the one employed by the Chronicler. Whatever the reason for the origin of the variant texts, it must be concluded that David's command to burn the idols with fire appeared *first* in the text of Samuel and that its presence in Chronicles MT says nothing about the bias or emphasis of the Chronicler.

1 Chr. 18:8
8a: And from Tibhath and from Cun, cities of Hadadezer, David took very much bronze;
8b: with it Solomon made the bronze sea and the pillars and the vessels of bronze.

2 Sam. 8:8
And from Betah and from Berothai, cities of Hadadezer, David took very much bronze.

Verse 8b in Chronicles has no parallel in Samuel MT. It is not legitimate, however, to interpret this as an addition by the Chronicler's hand, designed to accord with his view that David assembled all the raw materials for the temple before his death (see 1 Chr. 22:3), since a clause virtually identical with Chronicles MT appears already in the Greek text of Samuel. The Chronicler's "additional information" is merely a faithful rendering of an alternate copy of Samuel.

1 Chr. 18:4
And David took from him a thousand chariots, seven thousand horsemen and twenty thousand foot soldiers.

2 Sam. 8:4
And David took from him a thousand and seven hundred horsemen, and twenty thousand foot soldiers.

The Chronicler's mention of 1,000 chariots and 7,000 horsemen instead of the 1,700 horsemen in Samuel might indicate that he was multiplying numbers in order to make David's and God's victory over Hadadezer more impressive. This judgment is rendered unnecessary since the Chronicler's version of the numbers occurs in the Greek text of Samuel. The Chronicler again was following a text of Samuel different from MT, and perhaps superior to it.

1 Chr. 21:15b–16
And the angel of Yahweh was standing by the threshing floor of Ornan the Jebusite. *And David lifted up his eyes and saw the angel of Yahweh standing between earth and between heaven, and in his hand a drawn*

sword stretched out against Jerusalem. Then David and the elders, clothed in sackcloth, fell on their faces.

2 Sam. 24:16b
And the angel of Yahweh was by[24] the threshing floor of Araunah the Jebusite.

Since the italicized verse in Chronicles is contained in neither the Hebrew nor Greek texts of Samuel, most scholars have concluded that it was composed for this place by the Chronicler. Some have gone on to attribute the supraterrestrial location of the angel to the advanced angelology of the Chronicler. This judgment is rendered erroneous by the following copy of the Samuel passage discovered at Qumran:[25]

⌈And the angel of Ya⌉hweh was standing b⌈y the threshing floor of Arau⌉nah the Jebusite. And ⌈David⌉ lifted up⌈ his eyes and saw the angel of Yahweh standing between⌉ earth and between ⌈heav⌉en, and in his hand a drawn sword⌈ stretched out against Jerusalem. And David and the elders, covered with sackcloth, fell on their faces.⌉

However advanced an angelology the Chronicler may have elsewhere, this verse can no longer be used as additional supportive evidence. Instead, the Chronicler seems to have used here a copy of Samuel which already contained this verse.[26] What is more, Josephus paraphrases this verse in such a way that it is clear that he is following the text of Samuel and not that of Chronicles.[27] The Qumran-type text of Samuel, therefore, may have served as the basis for the Greek version used by Josephus. We must conclude that Josephus needs to be checked for important old Samuel readings elsewhere since they may be lost in other Greek and Hebrew witnesses.

2 Chr. 6:12–13
Then he [Solomon] stood before the altar of Yahweh, before the whole congregation of Israel, and he spread out his hands. *For Solomon had made a bronze platform and had set it in the midst of the court. Five cubits was its length and three cubits its height and he stood upon it. Then he knelt on his knees in the presence of the whole assembly of Israel and spread out his hands* to heaven.

24. The Hebrew word for "standing" was probably lost by homoeoarchton.
25. For a discussion of this text see F. M. Cross, Jr., *The Ancient Library of Qumran and Modern Biblical Studies* (Garden City, N.Y.: Doubleday and Company, rev. ed., 1961), pp. 188–191.
26. This verse may have been added to the Palestinian text of Samuel at an early date, or it may even be an original part of the text. A precipitating factor for the omission of this verse would be homoeoarchton (a scribe'ͤ eye skipped from "And David lifted up" to "And David said" in verse 17, thus omitting the verse in question).
27. Antiquities VII, 327–328.

1 Kings 8:22
Then Solomon stood before the altar of Yahweh, before the whole congregation of Israel, and he spread out his hands to heaven.

The additional, italicized material in Chronicles has been viewed by some as an attempt by the Chronicler to prevent Solomon from exercising priestly privileges—Solomon is said to pray from a bronze platform rather than from before the altar. Lemke saw, however, that the reason for the shorter text in Kings is homoeoteleuton: a scribe's eyes skipped from "and he spread out his hands" to "and he spread out his hands to heaven," thus leaving out everything in between. Since 1 Kings 8:54 implies that Solomon had been kneeling, the information provided now only by 2 Chr. 6:13 (Solomon knelt on his knees) is absolutely essential and must have once been included at the appropriate spot in 1 Kings 8:22. Even though all Greek and Hebrew evidence for this original reading in Kings has disappeared, it must be remembered that the Old Greek represents the text as it was transmitted in Egypt rather than in Palestine, and that the proto-Lucianic (Palestinian) recension can only be imperfectly reconstructed from our late Lucianic manuscripts.

2 Chr. 8
(No corresponding verse)

1 Kings 9:16
Pharaoh king of Egypt had gone up and captured Gezer and burnt it with fire, and had slain the Canaanites who dwelled in that city, and had given it as a dowry to his daughter, Solomon's wife.

While the Chronicler is considerably paraphrastic in the immediate context, some scholars have concluded that he omitted this particular verse because he considered it derogatory to the reputation of Solomon that an Egyptian Pharaoh would have conquered a city for him. As Lemke rightly observes, a person might equally well conclude that the Chronicler would have been delighted to include this information since it would illustrate that Solomon had so much power and prestige that an Egyptian ruler did favors for him. Lemke goes on to note, moreover, that the LXX of Kings omits all of verses 15–25 at this point although some manuscripts do include some of these verses after 10:22. Even there, however, verse 16 is only included in Hexaplaric manuscripts where it is identified as an addition from the Hebrew by an asterisk. The student is well advised, therefore, to refrain from *ad hoc* evaluations of the Chronicler's bias because of his omission of this verse—it probably was only added to the text of Kings long after the Chronicler wrote!

MORE SYNOPTIC PARALLELS

The purpose of studying the synoptic parallels between Samuel-Kings and Chronicles is not just to redefine or eliminate the biases of the Chronicler. Such study can also demonstrate the general accuracy of the textual theories which we are developing in this book. Since the Chronicler wrote in fourth-century Palestine, his copy of Samuel-Kings was not MT. Rather, it was that Palestinian type text which is attested from a later time at Qumran and which is closely allied to the Hebrew used by the first LXX translators. In the following pages, we will illustrate the decisive difference this approach makes in understanding the origin of readings in Chronicles.

2 Sam. 5:9 MT: And David built (it) round about. . . .
              LXX: And he built it a city round about. . . .[28]

1 Chr. 11:8 And he built the city round about. . . .

The LXX shows that the omission of "David" and the "addition" of the word "city" in Chronicles results from an alternate form of the text of Samuel rather than from the editorial hand of the Chronicler.

2 Sam. 5:10 MT: Yahweh God of Hosts
               LXX: the Lord of Hosts[29]

1 Chr. 11:9 Yahweh of hosts

The addition of "God" in Samuel MT is a frequent grammatical correction made by the scribes.[30] The Chronicler used a text of Samuel which had not been so emended.

2 Sam. 5:17 MT: And the Philistines heard that they had anointed David.
               LXX: And the *allophyloi*[31] heard that David had been anointed.

1 Chr. 14:8 And the Philistines heard that David had been anointed.

The Niphal form of the verb "anoint" in Chronicles was already present in the Hebrew text behind the Old Greek of Samuel, although

---

28. The difference between "it a city" in 2 Samuel LXX and "the city" in 1 Chronicles results from incorrect word division of the letters h'yr.
29. LXX's "Lord" (*kyrios*) represents Yahweh.
30. Proper nouns, like "Yahweh," cannot occur in the construct state.
31. A frequent LXX way of translating "Philistines."

attested now only in LXX. Samuel MT alone has the Qal form of the verb.

2 Sam. 6:5	MT:	And David and all the house of Israel were playing before Yahweh *with all the juniper trees.*
	LXX:	And David and the sons of Israel were playing before the Lord *with harmonized instruments, with power, and with songs.*
1 Chr. 13:8		And David and all Israel were playing before God *with all strength and with songs.*

Passing over the minor variants in the first part of these readings,[32] we can clarify the significant variations in the last part by studying the Hebrew (in transliteration):

2 Sam. MT: *bkl 'ṣy brwšym*
 LXX: *bkly 'z wbšyrym wb 'z*[33]

1 Chr. *bkl 'z wbšyrym*

As both Samuel LXX and Chronicles make clear, the MT's strange "juniper" results from an interchange (metathesis) of *š* and *r* in the original word "songs." The other change, from "strength" in Samuel LXX to "trees" in Chronicles, may have been precipitated in part by an effort to accommodate the text of MT to the secondary "juniper." In this case, Chronicles helps clarify the original reading in Samuel which would have been difficult to reconstruct from Samuel LXX alone because of its conflate character and strange translation patterns.

2 Sam. 6:6	MT:	And Uzzah stretched out toward the ark of God and he held it, for the oxen stumbled.
	LXX:	And Uzzah stretched out his hand toward the ark of God, to hold it, and he held it, for the oxen disturbed him, to hold it.
1 Chr. 13:9		And Uzzah stretched out his hand to hold the ark for the oxen stumbled.

Two readings are important here. First, the expression "his hand" in Chronicles is also attested in Samuel LXX and therefore it probably was in the Hebrew used for this translation. Secondly, the reason for the repetitious references to the verb "hold" in Samuel LXX can also

---

32. 2 Sam. MT: "all the house of"; 2 Sam. LXX: "sons of"; 1 Chr.: "all."
33. The rationale behind the LXX's strange translation is clarified by its handling of the similar verse 14.

be clarified through comparative study. There seem to have been two variant texts of Samuel:

Variant a: Uzzah stretched out his hand toward the ark of God and he held it. . . .

Variant b: Uzzah stretched out his hand to hold the ark of God. . . .

As far as this verb is concerned, Samuel MT is based on variant a, while Chronicles is based on variant b. Samuel LXX has a double reading. An "a" type reading has been expanded twice by insertion of a "b" type infinitive. Thus, these expansions confirm what might be guessed from the text of Chronicles, namely, that some Samuel manuscripts once had an infinitive, "to hold."[34]

2 Sam. 6:7   MT: by the ark of God
              LXX: by the ark of the Lord before God

1 Chr. 13:10   before God

Samuel MT and Chronicles are based on alternate, synonymous readings. Both readings have been conflated in Samuel LXX.

2 Sam. 6:9   MT: And he said
              LXX: saying

1 Chr. 13:12   saying

Without comparative study, the reading in Samuel LXX would be seen as slightly paraphrastic; so also the reading in Chronicles. But taken together, the readings show that there were probably Hebrew manuscripts of Samuel that read *l'mr* (saying) as well as MT's *wy'mr* (and he said).

2 Sam. 6:11   MT: And Yahweh blessed Obed-Edom and all his house.
              LXX: and the Lord blessed all the house of Obed-Edom and everything which belonged to him.

1 Chr. 13:14   And Yahweh blessed the house of Obed-Edom and everything which belonged to him.

An interesting variant in Samuel manuscripts can be isolated in these translations: (a) "everything which belonged to him"; (b) "all his house." Samuel MT preserves variant b in the final position; Chronicles preserves variant a.[35] In a sense, both of these Samuel

---

34. The omission of the final "to hold it" in many LXX manuscripts may be a correction to MT.

35. 1 Chronicles may be conflate like 2 Samuel LXX. But it reads the "house of" (Obed-Edom) instead of "all the house of."

variants have been conflated in Samuel LXX: variant a is left in the final position, and variant b is inserted before the name Obed-Edom.

All of the above examples have been based on comparisons between texts of Samuel and Chronicles. The following example differs, not only in that it compares Kings and Chronicles, but also in that it shows how the text of Lucian reflects the Palestinian text of Kings used by the Chronicler. In this case, the Old Greek is lost while Kings MT and LXX reflect a third family, perhaps from Babylon.

1 Kings 22:32 MT: And they turned against him to fight, and Jehoshaphat cried out.

LXX: And they surrounded him to fight, and Jehoshaphat cried out.

LXX^L: And they surrounded him to fight, and Jehoshaphat cried out, and the Lord saved him.

1 Chr. 18:31 And they surrounded him to fight, and Jehoshaphat cried out, and Yahweh saved him.

The initial verb apparently occurred in two forms in Kings manuscripts. "They turned against" (*wysrw 'lyw*) is found in the MT. "They surrounded" (*wysbw 'lyw*) is found in the LXX, proto-Lucian, and in the text of Kings used by the Chronicler. The expression "Yahweh saved him" in Chronicles is also based on a Kings Hebrew variant, preserved now only in translation in the Lucianic recension of LXX. It must be remembered that the LXX of 1 Kings 22 is part of the late, *kaige* recension. Its agreement in this case with MT is not surprising.

We hope that by now you are thoroughly convinced that the LXX does make a difference. The dramatic examples in this chapter are in some respects only the top of the iceberg. Icebergs can supply a lot of ice—and dangerous sailing for anyone who steers off course. It is now time to turn to the tools and techniques of textual criticism that will guarantee safe passage.

IV

The Greek and Hebrew Evidence

This chapter will survey the modern editions of the LXX, the important manuscripts and versions of the LXX, the problem of reconstructing the LXX text, and the evidence available to the textual critic of the Old Testament from Hebrew manuscripts and from versions based on the Hebrew.

THE EDITIONS OF THE LXX

The Old Testament in Greek according to the text of Codex Vaticanus (The Cambridge Septuagint).

Vol. I, *The Octateuch,* edited by Alan England Brooke and Norman McLean, contains i: Genesis, 1906; ii: Exodus, Leviticus, 1909; iii: Numbers, Deuteronomy, 1911; and iv: Joshua,[1] Judges, Ruth, 1917.

Vol. II, *The Later Historical Books,* edited by Alan England Brooke, Norman McLean, and Henry St. John Thackeray, includes i: 1 and 2 Samuel, 1927; ii: 1 and 2 Kings, 1930; iii: 1 and 2 Chronicles, 1932; and iv: Esdras, Ezra, Nehemiah, 1935.

Vol. III, containing i: *Esther, Judith, Tobit,* edited by Alan England Brooke, Norman McLean, and Henry St. John Thackeray, appeared in 1940.

In this edition the text of Codex Vaticanus is printed at the top of each page,[2] but the student should be aware that this text and the Old Greek are not identical. Although Vaticanus is the single

---

1. A superior edition of Joshua was prepared by Max L. Margolis, *The Book of Joshua in Greek,* parts I-IV (Paris: Geuthner, 1931–1938). Unfortunately the Introduction and the final part, covering 19:39ff were destroyed during World War II. The work was produced photographically from the author's hand-written copy.

2. Where Vaticanus has not been preserved (Gen. 1:1 to 46:8 and 2 Sam. 2:5–7 and 10–13) the text and the collations in the apparatus are usually derived from Alexandrinus.

best witness to the earliest form of the LXX in a number of books, it contains hundreds of secondary readings; in certain books, moreover, such as Deuteronomy and Chronicles, its text is relatively inferior. A critical text therefore must be reconstructed by each user of the Cambridge LXX since only the most obviously intolerable readings of Vaticanus have been corrected by the editors.[3]

Below the text of Vaticanus the editors supplied three sections of apparatus:

Apparatus 1. This section gives itacisms (see the Glossary) and other small errors of the principal manuscript adopted (that is, Vaticanus), plus those of a few other uncials.

Apparatus 2. This is the largest section of the apparatus. It gives the main variants in all the uncials known at the time of publication, in the group of cursives or minuscules selected for this edition, in the ancient versions of LXX, in Philo and Josephus, and in some early Christian writers who cited the Old Testament from a Greek version. It is in this apparatus that one finds readings from the cursives b, o, c₂, and e₂, the principal source of Lucianic (and proto-Lucianic) readings in Samuel and Kings.

Apparatus 3. Here is listed the evidence from the Hexapla, that is, readings from Aquila, Symmachus, and Theodotion and readings marked with the asterisks and obeli of Origen.

The principal value of this edition is that it collects a vast amount of evidence; this is also one of its weaknesses. As Ludwig Koehler once put it, "[The Cambridge LXX] gives all the material and is indispensable for the master mariner of LXX research; for the cabin boy, however, and also for the seaman, it is but a roaring sea of variants in which he perishes."[4] The all-too-brief introductions to the volumes of this edition can be supplemented and updated by the materials found in Jellicoe's *The Septuagint and Modern Study.*[5]

Septuaginta. *Vetus Testamentum Graecum auctoritate Societatis* (*Academiae*) *Litterarum Gottingensis editum.* (The Göttingen Septuagint.)

The Göttingen Septuagint includes the following Volumes: I, Genesis, edited by J. W. Wevers, in the press; VIII, 1:1 Esdras, edited by Robert Hanhart, in the press; VIII, 3: Esther, edited by Robert Hanhart, 1966; IX, 1:1 Maccabees, edited by Werner Kap-

---

3. Peter Walters (Katz) has offered the most detailed critique of this edition's editorial policies. See *The Text of the Septuagint,* ed. D. W. Gooding (Cambridge: At the University Press, 1973).
4. Quoted by Walters (Katz), *The Text of the Old Testament,* p. 2.
5. Pp. 269–296.

pler, 1936, 1967²; IX, 2:2 Maccabees, edited by Werner Kappler and Robert Hanhart, 1959; IX, 3:3 Maccabees; edited by Robert Hanhart, 1960; X; Psalms with Odes, edited by Alfred Rahlfs, 1931, 1967²; XII, I: Wisdom of Solomon, edited by Joseph Ziegler, 1962; XII, 2: Ecclesiasticus, edited by Joseph Ziegler, 1965; XIII; Minor Prophets; edited by Joseph Ziegler, 1943, 1967²; XIV: Isaiah, edited by Joseph Ziegler, 1939, 1967²; XV, Jeremiah, Baruch, Lamentations, Epistle of Jeremiah, edited by Joseph Ziegler, 1957; XVI, 1: Ezekiel, edited by Joseph Ziegler, 1952, 1967²; and XVI, 2: Susanna, Daniel, Bel, edited by Joseph Ziegler, 1954.

There are two major sections of apparatus in most volumes of the Göttingen Septuagint. The first contains the type of material found in apparatuses 1 and 2 of the Cambridge Septuagint. In addition to the fact that more manuscripts were available for this edition, the apparatus differs in two other essential ways: (1) the minuscules or cursives are identified by a number rather than a small Roman letter; and (2) the variants are ordinarily listed by groups or families.[6] This not only simplifies the listing in the apparatus, but it also graphically illustrates the distribution of a given variant and its importance. A critical use of this section of the apparatus enables the student to examine at first hand the recensional work on the LXX. The second section of the apparatus contains the hexaplaric material.

At the top of each page is printed a reconstructed text representing the Old Greek. The original plan, following Lagarde, was to reconstruct the recensions of Origen, Lucian, and Hesychius, and from them to establish the original LXX. While the complicated history of the LXX prevents a full realization of this goal, the reconstructed text nevertheless does represent the best possible approximation of what the Old Greek must have been.

Each volume in this series contains a very full introduction (in German), and the editors have also published monographs dealing with the individual problems in the books that have been published.[7] Jellicoe surveys the volumes of this edition with many helpful comments.[8]

6. There are six groups in Ziegler's edition of Jeremiah: the B-text, the A-text, the Q-text, the Hexaplaric text, the Lucianic text, and the Catena group.
7. See the extensive bibliography for Joseph Ziegler in Jellicoe, *The Septuagint and Modern Study*, p. 400. J. W. Wevers will publish a *Text History of the Greek Genesis* as vol. XI in *Die Mitteilungen der Septuaginta-Unternehmens der Akademie der Wissenschaften in Göttingen*.
8. *The Septuagint and Modern Study*, pp. 297–310.

*Septuaginta, id est Vetus Testamentum Graece iuxta LXX In-
terpretes.* Edited by A. Rahlfs. 2 vols. Stuttgart. Privileg. Württ.
Bibelanstalt, 1935.

This edition contains the entire Old Testament. Its reconstructed
text and the critical apparatus are based primarily on the fourth- and
fifth-century uncials Vaticanus, Sinaiticus, and Alexandrinus
although other sources, including the ancient versions of LXX, were
used occasionally. This "manual edition" can serve only a limited
purpose in textual criticism since the text is based on a very narrow
survey of the available manuscripts. Naturally the apparatus shares
the same limitations. The crucial evidence for the Lucianic manuscripts in Samuel-Kings, for example, is generally not presented. For
those who don't have access to Holmes and Parsons[9] or Swete,[10]
however, this edition provides the only text for books not yet published in the Cambridge or Göttingen editions. This includes Job,
Proverbs, Ecclesiastes, and Song of Songs.

Libri synoptici Veteris Testamenti. Edited by Primus Vannutelli. 2
vols. Rome: Pontifical Biblical Institute, 1931–1934.

This book prints out the parallel texts from Samuel-Kings on the
one hand and from Chronicles on the other. Isolated passages from
Psalms, Isaiah, and Jeremiah are cited where necessary. Vannutelli
prints the MT *and* LXX, including a fairly complete apparatus for
the latter. The relevant passages from Josephus and the Vulgate are
also included. This is a most useful tool for studying the textual problems that were illustrated in Chapters II and III.

SEPTUAGINT MANUSCRIPTS

Modern critical editions of the LXX can draw on hundreds of
manuscripts for collation and comparison. They are customarily
classified into three groups: papyri, uncial codices, and minuscules
or cursives.[11] We shall indicate briefly some of the more important
manuscripts in each category.

9. Robert Holmes and later James Parsons edited a five-volume critical edition,
Vetus Testamentum Graecum cum variis lectionibus (Oxford: At the Clarendon
Press, 1798–1827). See Swete, *An Introduction,* pp. 185–186 and Jellicoe, *The
Septuagint and Modern Study,* pp. 2–3.
10. H. B. Swete, *The Old Testament in Greek according to the Septuagint*
(Cambridge: At the University Press, 1887–1894). I: Genesis–IV Kings (1887;
1909[4]); II: 1 Chronicles–Tobit (1890, 1907[2]); III: Hosea–4 Maccabees,
Psalms of Solomon, Enoch, Odes (1894, 1912[4]). This work is sometimes called
the Cambridge *editio minor* to distinguish it from the larger Cambridge Septuagint.
11. By far the best account of these manuscripts in English is given by Jellicoe,
The Septuagint and Modern Study, pp. 175–242. He provides the date of the

Papyri

All of these are very fragmentary, but they also are the oldest witnesses to the text. Nearly seven hundred are known, dating to the seventh century and earlier.

Papyrus 967–968. This manuscript from the third century contains the Old Greek text of Daniel, known heretofore only in a tenth-century cursive and the Syro Hexapla.

Rylands Papyrus Greek 458. This is perhaps the oldest extant copy of the LXX, dating to the second century B.C.! It contains Deut. 23:24–24:3; 25:1–3; 26:12, 17–19; 28:31–33. Even after the discoveries at Qumran and elsewhere in the Judean desert, it remains one of the few pre-Christian copies of LXX.

Papyrus Fouad 266. This manuscript of the second or first century B.C. contains parts of Deuteronomy 18, 20, 24, 25, 26, 27, 31. One of its most interesting features is that the tetragrammaton is not rendered by *kyrios*, but instead by the Hebrew letters *y-h-w-h* in the so-called Aramaic script.[12] Attention should also be called to the Greek Minor Prophets scroll (R, see Chapter II) from the Judean desert, written on leather and dating to about the turn of the era, which formed a principal element in Barthélemy's isolation of the *kaige* recension. Papyrus fragments of Exodus 28 and Leviticus 2–5 and leather fragments of Leviticus 26 and Numbers 3–4—all dating to the first century B.C. or first century A.D.—have been discovered at Qumran.

Uncials

These manuscripts come from the fourth to the tenth centuries and have played a decisive role in reconstructions of the LXX text. Again only a few manuscripts of special interest will be listed here.

Codex Vaticanus (B). This fourth-century manuscript has often been taken as the best evidence for the prehexaplaric text. It underlies the editions of H. B. Swete, the Cambridge LXX, and, with Alexandrinus and Sinaiticus, the edition of Rahlfs. In certain respects, too much weight has been given to Vaticanus. Its text is inferior for Deuteronomy and Chronicles while in Isaiah it represents the hexaplaric recension rather than the Old Greek. Small sec-

---

manuscripts, the extent of their content, the textual family to which they belong, and voluminous bibliography.

12. This practice seems to lie behind the divine name *pipi* found in some LXX manuscripts. Presumably scribes transcribed the Hebrew letters written by the original translators into Greek letters which resemble them. Compare Swete, *An Introduction*, pp. 39–40.

tions of 2 Samuel, about thirty Psalms, and almost all of Genesis are missing from this manuscript.

Codex Sinaiticus (ℵ or S). This fourth-century manuscript was saved by A. C. F. von Tischendorf from destruction at St. Catherine's monastery on Mt. Sinai. The form of its text is related to B, but its orthography has been described as "careless." With the discovery of the papyri and other manuscripts, not so much weight must be placed on this and other early uncials. It lacks nearly the entire Pentateuch.

Codex Alexandrinus (A). This fifth-century manuscript is the only one of the three codices used by Rahlfs that contains most of the book of Genesis. Its text is quite eclectic with some books showing extensive influence from the hexapla. Because its text differs considerably from B in the Pentateuch, the editors of the Cambridge LXX erred when they used it for the text printed at the top of the page up to Gen. 46:28a, where B now begins. Lacunae occur in Genesis, 1 Samuel, and thirty Psalms are missing.

Codex Bodleianus (I). This ninth-century manuscript of the Psalms is noteworthy because marginal corrections have been inserted from Aquila, Symmachus, and Theodotion *and* from the so-called Quinta and Septima (see the Glossary).

Codex Marchalianus (Q). This sixth-century manuscript of the prophets is famous primarily for its copious marginal notes from Aquila, Symmachus, and Theodotion and diacritical symbols from the Hexapla.

Codex Washingtonianus (W). This papyrus codex of the Minor Prophets has been dated to the latter part of the third century. D. Barthélemy discovered that the first and second copyists who worked on this manuscript included many literalistic Hebraisms which appear to be drawn from the R-*kaige* recension.

Minuscules or Cursives

These are the latest of the manuscripts (dating from the ninth century and later), but they are of high importance. In many cases they represent copies (or copies of copies) of very old manuscripts. Thus while the manuscripts b, o, c_2, and e_2 come from the tenth-fourteenth centuries,[13] they are our only witness to the Lucianic

---

13. The editions of the Cambridge LXX adopted the use of small Roman letters to indicate the cursives. When they had exhausted the Roman alphabet, they began to go through it a second time. Hence a_2, b_2, c_2, etc. In Holmes and Parsons and the Göttingen edition, these Lucianic manuscripts are referred to by the numbers 19, 108, 82, 127, and 93 respectively; Jellicoe published two appendices showing how these sigla are used in the Cambridge LXX and com-

recension for Samuel and Kings which was made in the fourth century! The number of cursive manuscripts exceeds 1,500. The Cambridge LXX regularly cited about thirty-two of them; Ziegler's edition of Jeremiah in the Göttingen series used thirty-seven, with some assigned to each of his six families. Holmes and Parsons collated about three hundred!

ANCIENT VERSIONS OF THE LXX

Both the Cambridge and the Göttingen editions of the LXX contain numerous citations in their apparatuses from early translations of the Greek into other languages of the Christian church. These so-called daughter translations can be retranslated into Greek by modern scholars in order to supplement the evidence from the Greek manuscripts we have just surveyed.

We need this supplementary evidence because the extant Greek manuscripts have been corrupted by various kinds of editorial revision and by the accidental mistakes which are inevitable in any copying of manuscripts. While the daughter translations also show corruptions, some of them were made from Greek texts which had not undergone the Origenic or Lucianic revisions; others reflect the shape of the Greek text in a particular geographical locale. In any case, they are exceedingly old witnesses to the Greek text.

Except for the very advanced student, most people who use the critical editions of the LXX have to depend on the accuracy of the modern editors for collations of the secondary versions. Two major difficulties, however, make such collations subject to review: (1) Many of the daughter translations are available only in inadequate editions; that is, the many manuscripts of a given daughter translation have not yet been critically reconstructed, with the correction of internal problems. (2) The ancient translator may have produced a literal or free translation in the daughter language, or his exegetical opinions may have considerably affected how he translated the text. Despite these real difficulties, the daughter translations are extremely valuable; a few salient points about each will be noted in the following pages.

Old Latin or Itala. A number of independent translations into Latin were made by Christians in North Africa, Gaul, and the parts of Italy outside of Rome in the second century and later.[14] Because

---

paring the sigla in the Cambridge and Göttingen editions. Jellicoe, *The Septuagint and Modern Study,* pp. 360–369.

14. The Old Latin, which was translated from the LXX, is to be clearly distinguished from the later Vulgate, which was translated from Hebrew.

of this early date, many Old Latin texts are based on copies of the LXX that were still close to the Old Greek. Such Old Latin texts help modern editors to identify prehexaplaric readings in the Greek manuscripts that are extant and they even point to Greek readings not in any of the extant Greek manuscripts. In Samuel and Kings, the Old Latin is frequently evidence for the proto-Lucianic recension of the first century B.C. These translations survive in fragmentary manuscripts and in citations by the church fathers.[15]

Coptic. Coptic is the name given to various dialects of late Egyptian. The oldest translation into Coptic was done in the Sahidic dialect of upper Egypt (third century); the Achmimic and Bohairic are significant later Coptic versions. In the Minor Prophets, according to Barthélemy, the Sahidic seems to be a translation of the *kaige* recension rather than of the Old Greek.

Ethiopic. This Semitic version is thought to be a good witness to the unrevised (prehexaplaric) form of the LXX. It has affinities with Vaticanus in many books, although in Judges it follows the superior text type of Alexandrinus. It can sometimes be used to identify proto-Lucianic readings in Samuel-Kings.

Syro-Hexaplar. The Hexapla has been lost, but its fifth column has partially survived in a translation into Syriac made by Paul of Tella and others in 615–617. Called the Syro-Hexaplar for obvious reasons, this version is often our best witness to the content and critical markings (asterisks and obeli) of Origen's fifth column. Its translation of Daniel is based on the Old Greek which has been displaced by the recension of *kaige*-Theodotion in all but two of our Greek manuscripts.

The following versions are of markedly less importance: Gothic, Armenian, Georgian, Slavonic, and Arabic.

RECONSTRUCTING THE LXX

Modern editors of the LXX must reconstruct the original text, then, from a great many manuscripts, ancient versions, and citations by church fathers.[16] The Göttingen LXX's text, printed at

---

15. Pierre Sabatier collected the Old Latin remnants in a three-volume work of the eighteenth century. A twentieth-century edition is also in preparation although only Genesis has so far appeared. See Jellicoe, *The Septuagint and Modern Study*, pp. 249–251, for bibliography and special problems.

16. Evaluating the citations in the fathers is a very complicated task. On the one hand, verbatim citation was not regularly practiced, so that it is difficult to tell whether a given father is citing the LXX freely or whether he had a variant copy of the LXX. In addition, manuscripts of the fathers' writings were emended or miscopied by scribes over the years. Nevertheless, the fathers are

the top of the page, represents the fruits of such efforts: it is one of the great achievements of biblical research in the twentieth century. For books not yet edited in the Göttingen edition, the student can use Rahlfs' manual edition as a guide, or he can reconstruct the original LXX on his own on the basis of data supplied in the Cambridge LXX.

MANUSCRIPTS AND VERSIONS OF THE HEBREW BIBLE

In addition to the LXX and the Hebrew manuscript printed in *Biblia Hebraica,* the textual critic of the Old Testament must also utilize evidence from other Hebrew manuscripts and from other ancient translations of the Hebrew Bible.

Hebrew Manuscripts

Palestinian manuscripts. The decisive importance of the Qumran discoveries was surveyed in Chapter II. Additional manuscripts from Murabba'at and Masada are significant because they demonstrate that the wide variations in text types known from Qumran had disappeared by the end of the first century A.D. The excavations at Masada have uncovered an important Hebrew copy of Sirach. Patrick Skehan gives an excellent survey and analysis of these manuscripts in the *Jerome Biblical Commentary*.[17]

Samaritan Pentateuch. This recension of the Pentateuch, written in unpointed Hebrew, represents a late form of the expansionist, Palestinian text, and includes a series of sectarian readings inserted by the community centered at Shechem.[18] Because of the sectarian character of the Samaritans, the SP gives us a Hebrew witness independent of the changes that developed in mainline Jewish transmission, at least after about 100 B.C. It departs from MT in some 6,000 places and shares 1,600 of these variants with the LXX. The agreements between LXX and SP represent ancient Palestinian readings; that is, the Hebrew behind the LXX, before it was taken to Egypt, was part of the

---

occasionally the only or best witness to very important readings. Manuscripts whose texts agree with the Syrian fathers Theodoret and Chrysostum can often be assigned to Lucian. Barthélemy discovered that Justin Martyr followed the R-*kaige* recension in citing Micah 4:3–7. See the extensive comments by Swete. *Introduction* . . . , pp. 406–432, or any of the introductions to recent volumes of the Göttingen LXX.

17. See his article "Texts and Versions," pp. 563–566. Additional bibliography is given above in Chapter II, note 6.

18. See the discussion of SP in Chapter II and the reference there in note 9 to von Gall's edition.

Palestinian local text. At times these joint LXX-SP readings are original readings, now lost in MT; quite often they are secondary developments. They need to be evaluated individually. There are also Targums to SP and a Greek translation, the Samareitikon, which betrays the influence of the LXX.

Vocalized Hebrew manuscripts. In addition to the model codices listed at the beginning of Chapter II, there are many medieval manuscripts, including a number of manuscripts from the eighth to tenth centuries discovered in the Cairo Geniza. A collection of variants from medieval manuscripts and early editions was made by B. F. Kennicott and G. B. de Rossi in the late nineteenth century.[19] It should be noted, however, that the thousands of variants in these collections are of minor importance to the textual critic since most involve inconsequential spelling differences.

Ancient Versions of the Hebrew Bible

Targums. In post-exilic times the Bible was translated orally into Aramaic to meet the liturgical needs of the Synagogue. After centuries of oral and written transmission, these Targums[20] were reworked in the fifth century in Babylon to agree with the received text. Onkelos is the standard Targum for the Pentateuch while the Targum Jonathan is the standard for the prophets. The extant Targums for the Writings are generally thought to be of very late origin although older Targums were available as seen by the Targum of Job found in Qumran cave 11. Palestinian Targums on the Pentateuch[21] contain much additional narrative material, and they occasionally preserve older, non-Massoretic readings of the canonical text as well. In general the Targums are probably of more value for the history of exegesis and for the background to the New Testament than they are for strictly text critical study.[22]

---

19. Bibliographic references were given in Chapter II, note 4. A relatively neglected field has been the study of the variant citations of the Bible in the Talmud, Midrash, and other post-biblical Jewish writings. A preliminary analysis was made for Joshua, Judges, and Samuel by V. Aptowitzer, *Das Schriftwort in der Rabbinischen Literatur* (New York: KTAV, 1970; reprint of 1906 edition).

20. Targum is the Aramaic word for translation.

21. Such as Neofiti I, Pseudo-Jonathan, the Fragment Targum and fragments from the Cairo Geniza.

22. These investigations have been stimulated in recent years particularly in respect to Neophiti I. See Martin McNamara, *Targum and Testament* (Grand Rapids: William B. Eerdmans, 1972), and for secondary literature, Bernard Grossfeld, *A Bibliography of Targum Literature* (New York: KTAV, 1972).

Syriac. The Syriac version, the Peshitta, is a reworking of older Syriac translations. Scholars disagree on whether the first Syriac translations were made by Jewish or Christian communities, and they have not completely clarified the role of the Peshitta in the text critical enterprise. While individual variants are attested, the text base is Massoretic by and large. Corrections from the LXX have been inserted in the text, especially in Isaiah and the Psalms.[23]

Vulgate. Jerome translated the Hebrew Bible into Latin in the period between 389 and 405.[24] Previously he had revised the Old Latin (see above, under Ancient Versions of LXX) of the Psalter on two occasions (the *Psalterium Romanum* and the Gallican Psalter) and had even made a direct translation of it from the Hebrew (*Psalterium iuxta Hebraeos*). Since by the time of Jerome one stabilized consonantal text was standard, few major Hebrew variants can be identified or corrected on the basis of the Vulgate. Its primary value is for the history of exegesis.

23. A critical text of the Peshitta is now being prepared for publication under the leadership of P. A. H. de Boer. Called *The Old Testament in Syriac according to the Peshitta Version*, it will be published by E. J. Brill in Leiden.

24. Augustine objected strongly to Jerome's return to the Hebrew as a standard since the LXX was the inspired text of the church.

V

Doing Textual Criticism

A common mistake in Old Testament textual studies is to resort to LXX only when the MT, for one reason or another, seems difficult or corrupt. This procedure falls prey to two pitfalls: (1) The Hebrew text may have seemed difficult already to the translator. Consequently, a superior reading in LXX is not necessarily original; it may only result from the translator's glossing over a problem. (2) The LXX contains superior readings for passages in which the Hebrew is clear and in perfect order. Because of the existence of local texts and of extensive scribal reworking, the MT, though perfectly understandable, represents a variant and secondary form of the text. In this connection, the following warnings about use of the appartuses in *Biblia Hebraica* must also be issued:

The apparatuses do not cite all synonymous readings or all the evidence for shorter or longer readings. The reason for omitting some of the evidence for variants in LXX or the other versions may be related to the assumption that the MT is correct except where it is obviously difficult or corrupt.

The textual notes in the 1937 edition and in the current reissue are done by a great number of scholars whose presuppositions and assumptions vary and who are gifted with a wide range of text critical insight.

The notes and emendations are often focused only on one word or expression, thus neglecting the wider context in the LXX or other ancient versions.

The apparatuses in the 1937 edition contain errors of fact, as Harry M. Orlinsky has tirelessly pointed out.[1] Many emendations offered are merely conjectures, without manuscript or ver-

1. See "The Textual Criticism of the Old Testament," *The Bible and the Ancient Near East,* ed. G. Ernest Wright (Garden City, N.Y.; Doubleday and Company, 1961), pp. 113–132.

sional support. While conjectures are at times necessary, they are by definition the most subjective of operations. Especially suspect are those emendations made on the basis of an analysis of poetic meter (*metri causa*).

Insufficient account is taken of advances in Northwest Semitic philology, partly, of course, because most of these advances have been since 1937. A great number of proposed emendations have become unnecessary thanks to the work of W. F. Albright, Frank M. Cross, Jr., Mitchell Dahood, David Noel Freedman, Marvin Pope, and others.[2] In sum, *Biblia Hebraica* is a helpful collection of variants and scholarly suggestions, but it must be used critically. For valid textual criticism, the student must compare the entire Hebrew passage in question with the entire passage in LXX and the other versions.

To use the LXX in textual criticism, three basic steps are involved: (1) the original text of the version must be reconstructed; (2) those variations which were introduced by the translator himself must be eliminated; and (3) when it has been determined that the LXX translator knew an alternate Hebrew text, it must be determined whether his reading or that of MT is superior.

Since step 1 was treated in Chapter IV, this chapter will deal with the other two steps.

In step 2, the aim is to reconstruct the Hebrew text used by the first translator. The literalness of the vast majority of renderings facilitates this enterprise, even if this very literalness has led to the disparagement of the Greek style of the LXX ("translation Greek," "indifferent to idiom," "no rhythm"). The degree of literalness varies, from the slavish habits of Aquila and the rigid literalism of the *kaige* recension, to the somewhat freer style of the Old Greek itself. Within the latter category, of course, some translators are considerably more literal than others.[3]

In retroverting the Greek of the LXX into Hebrew, we must

---

2. For a brief discussion of this issue and bibliography on all the above names see Stanislav Segert, "The Ugaritic Texts and the Textual Criticism of the Hebrew Bible," *Near Eastern Studies in Honor of William Foxwell Albright*, ed. Hans Goedicke (Baltimore: Johns Hopkins Press, 1971), pp. 413–420. Methodological questions on the use of comparative philology need extensive debate before a consensus will be reached on many questions. See provisionally, James Barr, *Comparative Philology and the Text of the Old Testament* (Oxford: At the Clarendon Press, 1968).

3. Generally, the degree of literalness declines as we move from the Pentateuch, to the Prophets, and on to the Writings. Proverbs even has maxims of Greek origin!

make allowances for departures from strict literalism. The translators tended to amplify the text or omit minor expressions. At other times, they interpreted archaic or esoteric words. Instead of "I am uncircumcised of lips," one translator gave a non-literal approximation: "I am speechless." On the other hand, when the LXX reads "they saw the place where the God of Israel was standing" instead of MT's "they saw the God of Israel" (Exod. 24:10), we seem to have an example of the LXX's avoidance of anthropomorphisms. In all alleged non-literal translations, the question must always be raised whether these are in fact non-literal translations, or whether the translator had before him a text different from MT.[4] The replacement of "sons of God" by "angels of God" in Gen. 6:2 is typical of the freedom employed in translating some technical or metaphorical expressions. Finally, the LXX contains blunders due to a faulty Hebrew manuscript, misreading or misunderstanding the text, or inadequate knowledge of Hebrew.[5]

A recurring difficulty in retroversion is that a given Hebrew word can be translated by many different Greek words. Thus, the Hebrew word "to give" (*ntn*) is rendered by some thirty different words in the LXX. On the other hand, one Greek word can stand for several Hebrew words. A case in point is the verb *anapauesthai*, which is used by the translator of Isaiah for four different Hebrew verbs within seven verses (13:20–14:4)![6]

As a student compares the LXX and the Hebrew text, moreover, he must learn to identify whether apparent variations in LXX are due to real Hebrew variants or whether they are the results of the translator's "ineptitude" because of his exegetical, theological, or linguistic traditions. M. H. Goshen-Gottstein believes that rabbinic-style exegesis lies behind many apparent variations in LXX, and he has published an impressive series of

---

4. The so-called Princeton school (Henry Gehman, Donald Gard, Virgil Rogers, et al.) attributed many of the LXX's departures from MT to this or that theological bias. These efforts occasionally went to excess, partly because these scholars did not take seriously enough the possibility that a different Hebrew text was involved and partly because some of their generalizations were based on isolated examples.

5. The items in the preceding paragraph were treated in detail by Swete, *Introduction to the Old Testament in Greek*, pp. 325–330.

6. As Joseph Ziegler points out, the translator of Isaiah often reverted to a series of "stop-gap" words without any justification for this in the Hebrew text he was translating. In Isa. 33:1b, the translator apparently did not understand the Hebrew but composed a substitute sentence of his own using three of the stop-gap words. See his *Untersuchungen zur Septuaginta des Buches Isaias* (Münster: Verlag der Ashendorffschen Verlagsbuchhandlung, 1934), pp. 1–30.

readings from Isaiah LXX to demonstrate his point.[7] The new Hebrew University Bible Project will attempt to analyze LXX "variations" both through mechanical retroversion into Hebrew and through explaining their departure from MT as the result of Jewish interpretive processes. The reader will be called on to make the subjective choice between the two options.

A given translator's habits, including the consistency of his Hebrew-Greek equations must be checked through extensive use of Greek and Hebrew concordances. The Greek concordance to the LXX is usually referred to by the last names of its editors, Edwin Hatch and Henry A. Redpath.[8] It is based on words occurring in the three great codices, Alexandrinus (A), Vaticanus (B), and Sinaiticus (S), and on the Sixtine edition (largely Vaticanus) of 1587 (R). Minor attention is given to variant readings and the "later translators" (Aquila, etc.). The concordance does not list personal or relative pronouns, some conjunctions, and the definite article. For prepositions, only the biblical location is provided, without reproducing the actual text.

At the head of each article, the editors provide a list of Hebrew equivalents to the Greek word, drawn from a comparison with the MT. After each entry within the article, a number refers the reader to one of the Hebrew equivalents listed. If the editors were uncertain what Hebrew word lay before the translator, they indicated this by an obelus; a hyphen indicates there is no Hebrew equivalent.[9]

Another tool that would help identify Greek-Hebrew equivalents and the amount of freedom taken by the translators would be an up-to-date lexicon. Unfortunately, the standard lexicon is still that of J. F. Schleusner, first published in 1820–21. Lexicographical resources must be sought temporarily in the New Testament Lexicon of Bauer-Arndt-Gingrich, in Liddell and Scott, and in Lampe's *Patristic Greek Lexicon*. Bibliography on all the

7. See "Theory and Practice of Textual Criticism: The Text-critical Use of the Septuagint," *Textus* 3 (1963): 130–158. It should be remembered, of course, that conclusions based on the relatively free translation of Isaiah may not be valid for other books.

8. *A Concordance to the Septuagint and the Other Greek Versions of the Old Testament* (including the Apocryphal Books), 2 vols. (Oxford: At the Clarendon Press, 1897; with supplements, 1900–1906); reprinted in 2 vols. (Graz: Akademische Druck und Verlagsanstalt, 1954).

9. Sometimes the editors were uncertain because the free style of translation made a one-to-one equation impossible. At other times, they suspected that the translator's Hebrew text differed from MT. This part of the concordance has been subjected to sharp criticism, and a revision is being prepared by T. Muraoka.

lexicons can be found in Jellicoe, *The Septuagint and Modern Study*, pp. 335 and 374–375. A new lexicon is one of the major projects of the International Organization for Septuagint and Cognate Studies. A progress report and methodological debate has been published entitled *Septuagintal Lexicography*, ed. Robert Kraft (Missoula, Mont.: Society of Biblical Literature, 1972).

To illustrate the use of Hatch and Redpath in resolving the conflict between a mechanical and an interpretive understanding of a LXX variant, we may turn to a short phrase from 1 Chr. 16:10=Ps. 105:3: "(Let the heart of those who seek) Yahweh (rejoice)." The name Yahweh is regularly translated *kyrios* in LXX, and this is the case also here for Ps. 105:3 (LXX=104:3). But in Chronicles, we find the word *eudokia* instead, suggesting a translation: "(Let the heart of those who seek) his favor (rejoice)." The word *eudokia* occurs eight times in Psalms LXX, and its Hebrew equivalent in seven cases is identified by Hatch and Redpath as *rāṣôn*.[10] The translator of Chronicles uses the noun only here. Although one cannot generalize from the translation habits in one book to those of another, a tentative mechanical retroversion of Chronicles LXX would probably be *reṣônô*. Proponents of an "interpretive" understanding of the Greek "variant," on the other hand, might propose theological or exegetical reasons for the translator to give such a free rendering.[11] Fortunately, the subjective element in this case seems to have been eliminated by a discovery of a Qumran Hebrew fragment of Psalm 105 that read *rṣwnw* (=*reṣônô*) at this point![12] Before the discovery of this evidence, it would have been very difficult to defend a mechanical retroversion; now it seems assured.

Use of Hatch and Redpath, in any case, does provide a quick index to the way in which a given translator has used his Greek words. Whereas in 2 Chronicles a word like *eidolon*, though used only ten times, represents at least seven different objects of false worship in the Hebrew; at other times a translator's style will

---

10. The other case is marked with an obelus. In the second section of the supplement, Greek-Hebrew equivalents from Ecclesiasticus show the same translation habits although twice the noun is used there to translate a completely different Hebrew verb.

11. Hatch and Redpath indicated their own uncertainty by placing an obelus after the Chronicles reading.

12. The discovery of this fragment is full of mystery and intrigue. See Yigael Yadin, "Another Fragment (E) of the Psalms Scroll from Qumran Cave 11 (11QPsᵃ)," *Textus* 5 (1966): 1–10.

seem to be so consistent that when a variation in his choice of Greek words occurs, one is led to suspect that he knew a Hebrew reading different from MT (cf. the discussion of *eudokia* above). Through the index to Hebrew words published in the supplements to Hatch and Redpath, a student can determine all the Greek words that were used for any Hebrew equivalent throughout the LXX.[13] Students of Hebrew lexicography can be helped by this index to discover the denotations and connotations a given Hebrew word had for Greek-speaking Jews in the last centuries B.C. Investigation of Hebrew-Greek equivalents also offers dramatic evidence that the LXX was done by different translators. The word "Philistines," for example is transliterated in the Greek Hexateuch, but translated *allophyloi* (other tribes) in Judges and later books. Similar variation is shown when *sᵉbā'ôt* (hosts) is transliterated in Isaiah, but translated as *pantokratōr* (creator of everything) almost everywhere else.

Sometimes it is important to check how specific Hebrew forms or syntactical constructions are translated, and for this, a Hebrew concordance must be used.[14] Thus study of the frequent cliché *bᵉyny* has confirmed the notion that different sections of Samuel-Kings represent different translation techniques. The differing translations for this expression depend on two variables: whether the object of this phrase is Yahweh or a human being, and whether the expression occurs in the Old Greek or in the *kaige* sections of Reigns.

1. *bᵉyny* + a reference to God
   (a) in old Greek sections
       20 times = *enōpion*
       1 time = *en ophthalmois*

   (b) in *kaige* sections
       5 times = *enōpion*
       31 times = *en ophthalmois*
       1 time = *enantion*

13. Use of this index remains a rather tedious enterprise, however, since it only gives long lists of page and column numbers where the Greek equivalents can be found, instead of giving the Greek equivalents themselves. A replacement to this Hebrew-Greek index is being prepared for publication by T. Muraoka.

14. To investigate specific forms, prepositions, particles, interjections, and the like, see Solomon Mandelkern, *Veteris Testamenti Concordantiae* (Leipzig, 1896–1900; reprinted, New York; Schocken Books, 1962). To investigate nouns or verbs without regard to form, prefixes, suffixes, etc., see G. Lisowsky, *Konkordanz zum hebräischen Alten Testament* (Stuttgart: Privileg. Württ. Bibelanstalt, 1957).

2. *b'yny* + a human object
   (a) in Old Greek sections
   22 times = *en ophthalmois*
   10 times = *enōpion*
   1 time = *enantion*
   (b) in *kaige* sections
   16 times = *en ophthalmois*

The conclusions are obvious. *b'yny* is almost always translated by *en ophthalmois* in the *kaige* sections (forty-seven of fifty-three times). The translation is literal and consistent. The Old Greek, while not so consistent, seems to be operating according to two "rules": When *b'yny* is used with a human object, a variety of translations can be used—literal or free. When the expression is used with reference to the deity, however, the less literal expression *enōpion* is almost always employed.[15]

Similar studies with the expression "Thus says Yahweh," and with the word *'ēt* (time) in Jeremiah have turned up evidence for two different translators within one book. Up to chapter 29:7, "Thus says Yahweh" is translated consistently *tade legei kyrios* (about sixty times); thereafter, it is rendered *houtōs eipen kyrios* (about seventy times). Similarly *'ēt* is translated by *kairos* up until 28:18, but *chronos* thereafter. These and other studies have led to the convincing theory that the long book of Jeremiah was translated by two different people, with even a third hand being responsible for chapter 52.[16] Consequently, generalizations about the translator's style or method in the first half of the book may not apply to the style or method of the second half.

An index-concordance to the recension of Aquila is now available,[17] but a concordance to the rest of the Hexaplaric material can be found only in incomplete form in Hatch and Redpath (including both volumes and the supplements). A thorough modern index to the Hexaplaric material is being prepared by D. Barthélemy. Unfortunately, no one has yet met the crying need for an index to the Greek of Lucian, even for Samuel-Kings.

---

15. The statistics and conclusions are those of James Donald Shenkel, *Chronology and Recensional Development in the Greek Text of Kings* (Cambridge: Harvard University Press, 1968), pp. 14–17.

16. For these statistics and a table of Hebrew-Greek equivalences, see Henry St. John Thackeray, *The Septuagint and Jewish Worship* (London: Oxford University Press, 1923), pp. 116–117.

17. See Joseph Reider, *An Index to Aquila*, completed and revised by Nigel Turner, *Supplements to Vetus Testamentum* 12 (Leiden: E. J. Brill, 1966).

Determining the variations introduced by the translator himself is thus a complicated process. Not only must the student watch for paraphrastic style that presupposes no different Hebrew text, but he must also be aware that the translator's wide choice of vocabulary or his exegesis of the text may have led to "variations" that are only apparent. Finally, generalizations about one part of the Bible will not hold good for all books, or even necessarily throughout the book in question, since a variety of translators worked on the document we call the LXX. Nevertheless, when all variants attributable merely to the translator have been stripped away, the student is still left with a sizable number of readings where the LXX translators apparently used a Hebrew text that differed from MT.

WHICH READING IS TO BE PREFERRED?

While individual variant readings must be evaluated on their own merit, a general statement of the known relationship between the MT and the *Vorlage* of the LXX can be most useful in making textual decisions. Our comments on this relationship will be limited to the Pentateuch, Samuel, and Isaiah because of limitations of space and because our knowledge of this relationship is more precise in these books.

The Pentateuch

There are three principal text types for the Hebrew Pentateuch: (1) MT, (2) SP,[18] and (3) LXX. Because the text type found in SP is related to that cited by the Chronicler about 400 B.C. and to that documented in some of the Dead Sea Scrolls (4QPalaeoEx[m] and 4QNum[b]), this text type is assumed to be the Palestinian local text.[19] The LXX shows a relationship to this Palestinian text because of the 1,600 readings it shares with SP against MT. Nevertheless, LXX and SP have many differences both because of variants that arose during transmission of the Hebrew text after it was taken to Egypt and especially because of the extensive modifications and

---

18. For a statement of our position on the development of SP, see Chapter II.
19. The conclusions about local texts are those of Frank M. Cross, Jr. For a detailed statement of this point of view, see the following articles: "The Contribution of the Qumran Discoveries to the Study of the Biblical Text," *IEJ* 16 (1966): 81–95; and "The Evolution of a Theory of Local Texts," *1972 Proceedings of the International Organization for Septuagint and Cognate Studies*[2] (Missoula, Mont.: Society of Biblical Literature), pp. 108–126.

interpolations in the text that became SP. The MT had a separate history, perhaps in an isolated locale like Babylon.[20]

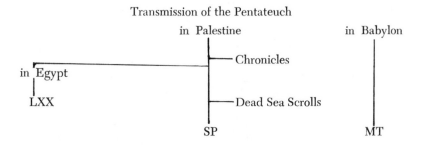

For some reason, the "Babylonian" text was eventually selected for the Pentateuch, and the Palestinian and Egyptian text types disappeared except for their preservation in the sectarian SP and in the LXX respectively.

Cross has described the MT in the Pentateuch as "a conservative, often pristine text, which shows little expansion and only a few cases of revision and modernizing." This is not to deny that hundreds of significant variants exist between MT and LXX (or SP). It should be noted that a reading attested in LXX and SP against MT is not necessarily superior, since LXX and SP are historically related and share a common origin in the Palestinian local text. They have many secondary readings in common, both in their "pluses" and in those constructions which are grammatically smoother. On the other hand, an agreement between LXX and MT against SP is considered very important because of the isolated development of these two text types.[21]

Samuel

Samuel MT is a poor text, marked by extensive haplography and corruption—only the MT of Hosea and Ezekiel is in worse condition. As the following diagram shows,[22] we now have access to two other local Hebrew texts; their character is different and often superior.

20. Cross has frequently urged a Babylonian setting although the argument is largely a process of elimination.
21. A reading in which SP and MT agree against LXX may only reflect late modification in SP.
22. Although the MT of Kings is not so corrupt as that of Samuel, the textual history of Samuel-Kings is otherwise closely related. Consequently, the rest of this section will deal with Samuel and Kings as one unit.

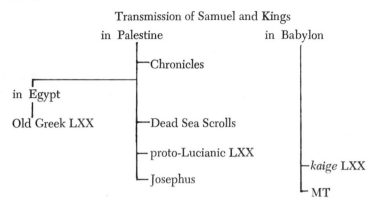

Transmission of Samuel and Kings

in Palestine — in Babylon

Chronicles

in Egypt

Old Greek LXX — Dead Sea Scrolls

proto-Lucianic LXX

Josephus

kaige LXX

MT

Whereas the LXX was a witness only to the Egyptian local text in the Pentateuch, a form of LXX corresponds to each of the three local texts in Samuel-Kings. The Old Greek LXX, preserved only in sections *a, bb,* and *gg,*[23] is fuller and often superior to MT. The *kaige* recension, extant only in sections *bg* and *gd,*[24] is based on an early (proto) form for MT.

The Palestinian local text is more closely allied to LXX than to MT. Access to each of our witnesses to it is beset with certain difficulties:

Chronicles is based on the Palestinian text of Samuel-Kings, but it is only an indirect witness to it since changes were introduced by the Chronicler as he prepared his new history.

The scrolls from Qumran (4QSam^{a,b,c}) are excellent witnesses to this text, but are preserved in a most fragmentary form.

Josephus used the proto-Lucianic recension, but only in the process of writing his own history; therefore, he is only at times a direct witness to the biblical text.

The proto-Lucianic recension itself is not preserved intact either. The church father Lucian revised this text toward MT in the fourth century. Because this revision was only partial, readings in the "Lucianic" manuscripts boc$_2$e$_2$ may be either proto-Lucian or Lucian.

Despite these difficulties with the witnesses to the Palestinian local text, authentic proto-Lucianic readings can still be isolated from our evidence according to the following formulae:[25]

Formula 1: Readings in which LXX^L and 4QSam agree while

23. *a*=1 Sam.; *bb*=2 Sam. 1:1–9:13; *gg*=1 Kings 2:12–21:43.
24. *bg*=2 Sam. 10:1–1 Kings 2:11; *gd*=1 Kings 22 and 2 Kings.
25. See Cross, "The Evolution of a Theory of Local Texts," p. 119.

MT and LXX^B have an alternate reading

(a) 1 Sam. 5:10 (section *a*)
    LXX^L and 4 QSam^a   the ark of the god of Israel
    MT and LXX^B   the ark of God
(b) 2 Sam. 24:18 (section *bg*)
    LXX^L and 4QSam^a   and he said
    MT and LXX^B   and he said to him

In both examples, LXX^L represents a proto-Lucianic revision toward the Palestinian Hebrew text known now through Qumran. These proto-Lucianic readings were not expunged in the later Lucianic revision. The Old Greek is still preserved by LXX^B in example "a", although LXX^B is part of the *kaige* recension in example "b."[26]

Formula 2: Readings in which 4QSam, MT, and Josephus agree while LXX^B has an alternate reading

It might be argued that Josephus, who usually cites the Bible from the "LXX," adjusted his text in such cases to agree with the MT. But the Qumran evidence suggests that he had access to a Greek text that had been revised to agree with the Palestinian Hebrew. That is, his reading is proto-Lucianic.

Formula 3: Readings in which 4QSam and Josephus agree while LXX^B and LXX^L and MT have an alternate reading

For example, 4QSam^a and Josephus contain a paragraph before 1 Sam. 11:1 describing an earlier, otherwise unknown campaign against Nahash, king of Ammon. This paragraph has been lost in MT and LXX^B and L.[27] Josephus had access to a proto-Lucianic Greek text which still contained it; our present Lucianic manuscripts, however, have lost it because of Lucian's corrections toward MT.

We can conclude that the MT of Samuel is very corrupt, but its reconstruction is facilitated by our access, both direct and indirect, to two other local text traditions from Egypt and Palestine. Three ways to uncover authentic proto-Lucianic or Palestinian readings

26. It is impossible to be sure whether LXX^L is proto-Lucianic or Old Greek in example "b." Perhaps the Qumran reading, however, tilts the decision toward a proto-Lucianic interpretation.
27. A corrupt passage in 1 Sam. 10:27b MT, which refers to the content of this paragraph, demonstrates that the paragraph was original.

from our fragmentary evidence have been outlined in our discussion of formulas.[28]

Isaiah

With most of the prophets, there are only two types of text extant: MT and LXX. In Jeremiah and Ezekiel, these two types diverge dramatically; MT is a full, expansionist text and the LXX a shorter, more original one.[29] The LXX in Isaiah, though belonging to a different textual tradition than MT, shares some of the latter's expansionist attributes. In addition, some seventeen Hebrew manuscr pts from Qumran, dating over a period of two and one half centuries, are all expansionist. Since the expansions in MT, LXX, and the Qumran scrolls are not always at the same places, we are given some data by which to identify additions that have been made. As we have seen, however, quite severe problems can be expected by the student in using the LXX as a text critical tool in Isaiah. The Hebrew vocabulary of Isaiah is rich and difficult for the modern reader, and would have been also for the LXX translator. Since the translator displays a tendency to be free and paraphrastic, it is occasionally difficult to be sure what his Hebrew text read.

CHOOSING THE CORRECT READING

When it comes to deciding between individual Hebrew readings, the critic is both scientist and artist: his decision will depend on knowledge of the essential data, but it will also reflect his own skill as a text critic. Such "art" can be learned or at least developed by study and practice. One way to accomplish this is to read acknowledged masters in the field, like Julius Wellhausen or S. R. Driver,[30] and ask what factors made them decide for one variant over

28. In my doctoral dissertation, I compared 1 Esdras, which contains translations of 2 Chronicles 35–36, Ezra 1–10, and Nehemiah 8, with another translation of these chapters in LXX. The thesis demonstrated that 1 Esdras represents a more original form of the text. In almost seventy readings, a Hebrew or Aramaic expression omitted by 1 Esdras is also omitted by LXX, by the Syriac, or by the corresponding text in the Deuteronomistic history. Agreements of 1 Esdras with the text of Nehemiah against the text of Ezra in Ezra 2/Nehemiah 7 (the parallel list of returnees) demonstrate further the reliability of 1 Esdras. Nearly a score of conflations in MT and numerous other additions from the context were detected via 1 Esdras alone. Second-century Egypt seems to be the time and place for the origin of 1 Esdras; LXX, with its highly expanded proto-Massoretic text type, is Palestinian and typologically later than 1 Esdras. Cf. my notes and articles in *HTR* 59 (1966): 449; 60 (1967): 93–105; 61 (1968): 492–495; and 62 (1969): 99–107.

29. Extensive treatment of the text of Jeremiah was provided in Chapters II and III.

30. Bibliographical references can be found in Chapter III, note 2.

another. These two scholars combined fine textual skills with penetrating insight into the exegetical questions involved in the passage itself and with comprehensive knowledge of the style of the biblical authors. One will soon recognize the subjective nature of their decision-making process and will see where solutions other than theirs might be possible and even more likely. At the same time, both Wellhausen and Driver often cut through centuries of emendations with a brilliant new synthesis of the data or a compelling conjecture that should alert and prepare the student for the infinite problems that confront a textual historian. Even the beginner, however, can make reasonable and proper decisions by weighing evidence according to the following criteria.

External Considerations

Manuscripts are weighed, not counted. So goes an old maxim about textual criticism. It means that not every manuscript or version is of equal value and that ten copies of a bad manuscript do not make it original. A variant that occurs in the Dead Sea Scrolls, the Samaritan Pentateuch, or LXX will probably be given more attention than if it appears in a Targum or in one of the daughter translations of the LXX. If the variant occurs in two or more manuscripts or versions, it grows in importance. Nevertheless, the MT itself deserves very high respect and should be changed only with great caution. In cases where the criteria listed below under internal considerations are indecisive, the student is well-advised to prefer the MT.[31] Since all manuscripts and versions contain mistakes, a student would be led to disastrous mistakes if he followed only external criteria. Therefore, in every case, the decision should rest primarily on the inherent value of the variant readings themselves.

Internal Consideration

Choose the reading which best explains the origin of the others.

It is often possible to reconstruct the origin of a variant and to detect the accident or the intervention of a scribe that caused it. In 1 Sam. 16:5, we find the following variants:

MT: (Sanctify yourselves and) come (with me) to the sacrifice.
LXX: (Sanctify yourselves and) rejoice (with me) today.

---

31. The following relative order of importance was proposed by Ernst Würthwein: MT, SP, LXX, Aquila, Symmachus, Theodotion, Syriac, Targum, Vulgate, Old Latin, Sahidic, Coptic, Ethiopic, Arabic, Armenian. See *The Text of the Old Testament*, trans. Peter R. Ackroyd (New York: Macmillan Company, 1957), p. 76.

The variation was clearly not caused by miscopying letters that looked alike. Rather, someone chose to substitute one reading for another. In our opinion, the reading now preserved by the LXX was original; it left ambiguous why the people were to sanctify themselves. Therefore, the secondary MT arose *because* a scribe wanted to remove the ambiguity in the Hebrew text. If the MT were to be the original reading, on the other hand, we can think of no compelling reason why the LXX reading would have been substituted.

The shorter reading is to be preferred.

Unless there is clear evidence for homoeoteleuton or some other form of haplography, a shorter text is probably better. The people who copied manuscripts expanded the text in several ways: they made subjects and objects of sentences explicit whereas they were often only implicit in the original text; they added glosses or comments to explain difficult words or ideas; and when faced with alternate readings in two or more manuscripts they were copying, they would include both of them (conflation) in a serious attempt to preserve the original. While some scribes may have abbreviated from time to time, we believe that the interpretation of a shorter reading as abbreviation should only be chosen as a last resort.

The more difficult reading is to be preferred.

Grammatical, historical, theological, and lexical difficulties often were eliminated or modified by the scribes as they copied the manuscripts. The scribes would not knowingly insert a more difficult form for a common one or an archaic or rare word instead of one in everyday usage. A rigid use of this rule, of course, would lead to the reconstruction of a text full of copyists' mistakes! Our increased knowledge of Hebrew and of the Northwest Semitic languages, however, usually makes it possible to decide if a strange spelling is truly archaic and genuine, or if it is only a slip of a copyist's pen.

A thorough acquaintance with the common causes of textual error in Hebrew manuscripts, as outlined in the following paragraphs, will prepare the student to detect and evaluate such errors.

It must be stressed, however, that many variants are unique. After all, expressions were at times omitted for no apparent reason, and not all variants in spelling, grammar, or vocabulary are easily classifiable.

COMMON TYPES OF ERRORS IN HEBREW TEXTUAL TRANSMISSION

The following categories of textual error are meant only to be illustrative. Other categories could be cited and many variants fit none of our categories, but are the product of a careless, fatigued, or merely fallible scribe.

Unintentional Changes

These variations arose because the scribe read, wrote, or heard the text incorrectly.[32]

Confusion of letters which look alike

The similarity of the letters *daleth* and *resh* led to the confusing of the countries Aram (*'rm*) and Edom (*'dm*) in Hebrew manuscripts. Even in 1 Sam. 14:47, where all manuscripts and versions read "Edom," the editors of *Biblia Hebraica* suggest a change to Aram.[33]

A slightly different kind of mistake is represented by variants in 1 Sam. 17:32:

MT: heart of man (*'dm*)
LXX: heart of my lord (*'dny*)

Apparently, the final *ny* of "my lord" was misread as a final *m* in MT.

A misreading of the consonants *w* and *r* produced quite divergent texts in 1 Sam. 14:47:

MT: he pronounced (them) wicked. (*yršy'*)

LXX: he was victorious. (*ywš'*)

Other common confusions in the so-called square of Aramaic script involve *b/k*; *h/ḥ*; *h/t*; and *w/y*.[34]

Confusion of words which sound alike

Mistaken hearing can be illustrated by the interchange in manuscripts between "to him" (*lô*) and "not" (*lō'*). An error in hearing also led to a difference in 1 Sam. 28:2, where LXX has "now" (*'attâ*) and MT has "you" (*'attâ*). Compare also the MT in 1 Sam. 22:13,

32. Manuscripts were sometimes copied by a scribe from another manuscript that lay before him. At other times, a group of copyists would write as the manuscript was read aloud.
33. This conjecture is partially supported by the addition of the words "Beth Rehob," an Aramean (1) city, in LXX[L] at this point.
34. For examples of each of these, see Ernst Würthwein, *The Text of the Old Testament*, p. 72.

which can be translated "he has risen against me, to lie in wait," with the LXX which must be rendered as "he has risen against me, as an enemy." In Hebrew, this represents only the difference between *leʾōrēb* (MT) and *leʾōyēb* (in the Hebrew text used for LXX).

Omission because of homoeoteleuton (=similar ending)

When two words occur in a passage with similar or identical endings, the eyes of the scribe sometimes skipped from the first to the second and left out everything in between. Below are translations of LXX of 1 Sam. 13:15 and 2 Sam. 14:30. In each case, the italicized words have been lost by homoeoteleuton in MT.

1 Sam. 13:15: And Samuel arose and set out from Gilgal *and went on his way; but the rest of the people went up after Saul to meet the soldiers. Then they came from Gilgal* to Gibeah of Benjamin.

2 Sam. 14:30: And so Absalom's servants set the field on fire. *The young men of Joab came to him with torn garments and reported that the servants of Absalom had set the field on fire.*[35]

Omission because of homoeoarchton (=similar beginning)

Words that began in the same way sometimes led a copyist's eyes to skip from the first occurrence to the second, leaving out everything in between. This happened somewhat less frequently than homoeoteleuton. Examples from 1 Sam. 10:1 and 29:10 were discussed in Chapter III.

Haplography (=single writing)

Strictly speaking, this refers to the single writing of two letters or words which appear together, but it is also used to refer to any accidental omission of letters or words.

1 Sam. 16:7
LXX: "Not as man sees, does God see." (This presupposes a Hebrew reading: *lʾ kʾšr yrʾh hʾdm yrʾh hʾlhym.*)
MT: (Omits the last two words by haplography).

1 Sam. 17:8
LXX: choose (=bḥrw)
MT: (The text is haplographic; it omits the letter ḥ.)

1 Sam. 17:46
LXX: "I will leave *your corpse and the* corpses of the Philistine army." (The italicized words presuppose a Hebrew text: *pgrk wpgry.*)
MT: (For the words in question, MT has only *pgr.*)

---

35. The italicized words are also in 4QSamᶜ according to NAB.

Sometimes the omission does not involve words which look alike. In the following translation of LXX, the italicized words have been lost by sheer accident in MT.

1 Sam. 12:9
LXX: "captain of the army of *Jabin king of* Hazor."

Dittography (=double writing)

In 1 Sam. 15:32, the RSV reads: "Surely the bitterness of death is past"; NAB has: "So it is bitter death." The difference represents a text-critical change. The editors of NAB recognized that the word translated "is past" in RSV (*sr*) is really only a partially miswritten dittograph of the word "bitter" (*mr*). Their judgment is supported by the omission of the word *sr* in LXX and 4QSam^a.

In Ezek. 48:16, the dimensions for the south side of the city are given as "five five hundred and four thousand cubits." The Massoretes recognized the difficulty with the double "five" and did not vocalize its second occurrence, thus indicating that it was not to be read.

2 Sam. 6:3–4: "And they made the ark of God ride on a new cart, and they took it away from the house of Abinadab which is on the hill. Uzzah and Ahio, sons of Abinadab, guided the *new* cart, *and they took it away from the house of Abinadab which is on the hill.*"

The italicized words are a double writing, repeating the words which followed the first mention of the word "cart" (according to the Hebrew word order in which adjectives follow nouns). This analysis is supported by 4QSam^a, the LXX, and by the grammatical difficulty this repetition caused in Hebrew.[36]

Incorrect word division

This mistake is more common in Greek manuscripts in which words were written without intervening spaces, but it was possible also in Hebrew before vocalization took place. The difference in the following passages depends on whether the letter *h* is treated as the suffix of the verb or the definite article on the following noun:

2 Sam. 5:9–LXX: And he built it a city (=*wybnh 'yr*)
1 Chr. 11:8–MT: And he built the city (=*wybn h'yr*)

---

36. The word "new" does not have the definite article. This, of course, is correct the first time it occurs in our passage. In its second, dittographic position, however, the adjective needs the article to agree with the noun it modifies.

Incorrect vocalization

The vowel markings (points) were first added to the text in the sixth to ninth centuries A.D. They record a traditional pronunciation which at times is mistaken. Thus in 1 Sam. 18:11, the first verb was pointed *wayyāṭel* ("and he cast") by the Massoretes,[37] but the LXX translator understood the consonantal text as if it were vocalized *wayyiṭṭōl* ("and he picked up"). The LXX understanding is probably superior although both readings are possible.

Metathesis or accidental transposition of words or letters

1 Sam. 14:30
MT: today the people
LXX and 4QSamᵃ: the people today

The notes in NAB suggest that the latter is correct.

1 Sam. 22:23 Whoever seeks my life seeks your life.

While there is no manuscript evidence, it is commonly recognized that the correct reading should be: Whoever seeks your life seeks my life (NEB and NAB, but not RSV).

1 Sam. 30:19
MT: to sons or daughters and from booty
LXX: and from booty (and) to sons or daughters

The awkward MT is probably the result of metathesis.

1 Sam. 17:39
MT: and he endeavored unsuccessfully (=*wy'1*).
LXX: and he exerted himself (=*wyl'*).

The translation suggested for MT is a forced and problematic interpretation of the verb in Hebrew. It is better to suppose that MT has been corrupted by metathesis.

Ps. 50:20: You sit (*tšb*), you speak with your brothers.

According to a conjecture in the new edition of *Biblia Hebraica,* it would be better to read: "you speak shameful things (*bšt*) with your brothers." The difference is only one of letter order.

37. MT parsed the verb as if it came from *ṭwl*; LXX derived it from *ntl.*

Substitution of synonymns

At times, this may have been an unintentional change as the
scribe's memory slipped from the time he saw or heard the passage
until the time he wrote it down.

1 Sam. 10:25
MT: each man to his home
LXX and 4QSam[a]: each man to his place[38]

*Assimilation of the wording in one passage to the slightly differ-
ent wording in the context or in a parallel passage*

1 Sam. 12:15—MT: the hand of Yahweh will be against you and your
           fathers.

The inclusion of the word "your fathers" gives an unsuitable sense;
the original reading may have been "and your king," now attested
only by LXX[L]. As S. R. Driver suggested, the word "fathers" may
have resulted accidentally because of the frequent mention of
"fathers" in verses 6–8 of the same chapter.

*Mistaken inclusion of marginal or interlinear comments into the
text*

The following example was originally published by Shemaryahu
Talmon:[39] Isa. 24:4—MT: the "heights" with the land (mourn). The
original writer of 1QIs[a] wrote: *mrwm h'rṣ=* the height(s) of the
land (mourn). Above the line in 1QIs[a], a scribe wrote the word *'m*
(=people). Talmon believes this word was part of an alternate
form of this line: "the people of the land (mourn)." At a subsequent
copying of this manuscript, the interlinear *'m* was inserted into the
text where it had to be construed as the word "with," whose consonantal spelling is identical with "people."[40]

Intentional Changes

For various reasons, scribes tried to correct what appeared to
them as corruptions, and in the process they produced textual
change.

38. Shemaryahu Talmon has published extensively on such variations. See
"Synonymous Readings in the Textual Traditions of the Old Testament,"
Scripta Hierosolymitana 8 (1961), pp. 335–383.
39. "Aspects of the Textual Transmission of the Bible in the Light of Qumran
Manuscripts," *Textus* 4 (1964): 118.
40. For a similar confusion of *'m*, the preposition, with *'m*, a noun meaning
"people," see 2 Sam. 10:6 LXX; cf. 1 Chr. 19:6.

Changes in spelling or grammar

Subjects and verbs were often made to agree exactly in person or number. Conjunctions, the word "all," and other minor additions were made from time to time.

Harmonizations

The following quotation of David provides an example:

1 Sam. 20:5
MT: Let me hide in the open country until the third evening.
LXX: Let me hide in the open country until evening.

The addition of the word "third," which is grammatically difficult, seems to be an attempt to harmonize with verses 34–35 where we are informed that David actually remained in hiding until the third day.

Conflation of variant readings

A scribe might include variants attested in separate manuscripts, not realizing only one of them was original.

Ezek. 1:20 Wherever the spirit wanted to go, they went, *wherever the spirit wanted to go,* and the wheels rose along with them.

The italicized expression is lacking in some Hebrew manuscripts, LXX, and Syriac. Apparently, there were two forms of this phrase (*šm hrwḥ llkt and šmh hrwḥ llkt*), both of which were conflated in MT.[41]

Filling out of names and epithets

Examples of this were included in our discussion of the Hebrew text of Jeremiah in Chapter III.

Supplying subjects and objects

Explicit mention of the sentence subject or object was often lacking in the original. As the text was transmitted in Hebrew and translated into other languages, proper names were inserted or substituted for pronouns. Occasionally, different subjects or objects were included in separate manuscripts. Wellhausen formulated a rule that "if LXX and MT differ in respect of a subject, it is probable that the original text had neither."[42]

---

41. The variant would have arisen by dittography or haplography of *h*.
42. Quoted by Driver, *Notes on the Hebrew Text,* p. lxii.

Expansions from parallel passages

We have already called attention to such expansions from parallel passages within Isaiah in 1QIs^a (Chapter II), to glosses in Jeremiah MT from other biblical books (see 28:16, 29:32, 48:45–46; and above Chapter III), and to the abundant examples of this from the Samaritan Pentateuch and the Palestinian local text type in general. The Decalogue, which occurs in two recensions in the Bible, was naturally a prime target for such harmonization. Whereas the MT has different rationales for keeping the Sabbath commandment in Exod. 20:11 and Deut. 5:14–15, a Qumran document, 4QDtⁿ, inserts the rationale from Exod. 20:11 after Deut. 5:15.[43]

Removal of difficult expressions

Certain matters of history, geography, or theology seemed incorrect or even offensive to the copyists and were corrected. Attention is frequently called to Job 1:5, 11 and 2:5, 9 where the expression to "curse God" has been replaced in all texts by the euphemism to "bless God." The original text of Gen. 18:22 seems to have read: "And Yahweh was still standing before Abraham," but since "standing before" can mean "worship," early copyists changed the text to read, "Abraham was still standing before Yahweh."[44]

In the following example, the LXX seems to preserve the original reading; the italicized words in MT were inserted by a scribe who apparently feared that the curse might recoil on the Davidic line since David had never carried out his threat:

1 Sam. 25:22
MT: May God do thus and so to *the enemies of* David if by morning I leave a single male alive.
LXX: May God do thus and so to David if by morning I leave a single male alive.

Replacement of rare words with more common ones

1 Sam. 20:34
MT: Jonathan rose (*wyqm*)
LXX and 4QSam^b: Jonathan sprang up (wyphz)

The MT seems to represent a replacement of the rare verb used in the original Hebrew text.

43. A similar harmonization occurs in LXX^B of Deut., but there it appears between 5:14 and 5:15.
44. This is one of the eighteen "corrections of the scribes" which were already identified by the Massoretes.

Isa. 39:1
MT: (Hezekiah) became well (*wyḥzq*)
1QIsᵃ: (Hezekiah) became well (*wyḥyh*)

In this reading, MT contains the rarer form; a more common vocable has been inserted in the Qumran text.

Textual criticism is only one of the methods necessary for understanding the message of the Bible. In addition, the student must learn the techniques of translation and lexicography, of form, tradition, and redaction criticism, of word study, and of historical reconstruction. Most exegetes do textual criticism as only one of their interests; few have the leisure to devote full time to this enterprise. No exegete, however, dare ignore it.

As all the tools and techniques of biblical exegesis are utilized, tentative textual judgments may require modification. Knowledge of the overall message of a writer, his style, and his other distinctive traits must be considered in any final textual decision. While we live in an age of specialists and specialization, the specialists must listen to what scholars in related areas of their discipline are saying. Biblical exegetes must be in dialogue with philosophers, ancient and modern historians, sociologists, anthropologists, systematicians—and with each other.

The textual critic in the last quarter of the twentieth century will be affected in any case by Qumran. He will be wary of those generalizations, still published in the 1970s, which assure the reader that "Qumran has shown that the Massoretic text of Isaiah is attested already in the first century of our era," or that "at Qumran, one is struck by the observation that the Pentateuch there was Massoretic." Neither generalization tells the whole truth. The Qumran Isaiah fragments are much like Isaiah MT, but by no means identical with it. In addition, neither the Qumran manuscripts of Isaiah nor the MT are the original text; they are witness to its early expansion. The conservative text of the Pentateuch contained in the MT is indeed preserved by the Judean scrolls, but so is an expanded, Palestinian local text, sharing many traits in common with the Samaritan Pentateuch.

The emphasis on change, variants, and corruptions in this book should not dull our appreciation for those anonymous copyists of ancient times who tirelessly preserved the text for us. A large proportion of the words of the Bible are unanimously attested by ancient Hebrew manuscripts, the LXX, and the other versions.

When variants do occur, we can use well-informed methodology to sort through and evaluate the available evidence. Textual problems become opportunities for new and better understanding of the texts themselves and the communities which transmitted them.

Textual criticism, as we said in the Preface, is the discipline that tries to recover the original copy of a piece of literature. That major goal should perhaps be qualified. At times we may want to reconstruct not only the autograph, but also the type of text preserved in Palestine or some other locality. These reconstructed local texts may well help to clarify how the writer of Chronicles or the book of Jubilees went about his business of rewriting older documents, such as the books of Samuel and Kings or the Pentateuch.

Finally, this book is an invitation to begin. Much remains to be done, not only by specialists who spend their lives evaluating ancient manuscripts and versions, but also by the average exegete, pastor, rabbi, theological student or informed lay person, who wants to find out more about how the Bible came to us.

Selected Bibliography

BROCK, SEBASTIAN P., Fritsch, Charles T., and Jellicoe, Sidney. "A Classified Bibliography of the Septuagint." In *Arbeiten zur Literatur und Geschichte des Hellenistischen Judentums VI*. Leiden: E. J. Brill, 1973. This book provides access to most of the scholarly literature on the LXX from about 1860 to 1969.

JELLICOE, SIDNEY. *The Septuagint and Modern Study*. Oxford: At the Clarendon Press, 1968. Jellicoe's introduction is supplementary to Swete and brings the discussion up to date, without repeating all the basic information contained in the previous work.

———. *Studies in the Septuagint: Origins, Recensions and Interpretations*. New York: KTAV, 1973. These selected essays supplement Jellicoe's earlier monograph.

OTTLEY, R. R. *A Handbook to the Septuagint*. London: Methuen and Company, 1920.

SWETE, HENRY BARCLAY. *An Introduction to the Old Testament in Greek*. Revised by R. R. Ottley. Cambridge: At the University Press, 1914.

The latest developments in LXX research are reviewed each year in the *Bulletin of the International Organization for Septuagint and Cognate Studies*.